Strangeways
A Century of Hangings in Manchester

FOUL DEEDS AND SUSPICIOUS DEATHS Series

Wharncliffe's *Foul Deeds and Suspicious Deaths* series explores, in detail, crimes of passion, brutal murders and foul misdemeanours from early modern times to the present day. Victorian street crime, mysterious deaths and modern murders tell tales where passion, jealousy and social deprivation brought unexpected violence to those involved. From unexplained death and suicide to murder and manslaughter, the books provide a fascinating insight into the lives of both victims and perpetrators as well as society as a whole.

Other titles in the series include:

Foul Deeds and Suspicious Deaths in Birmingham, Nick Billingham
ISBN: 1-903425-96-4. £10.99

Foul Deeds and Suspicious Deaths in Bolton, Glynis Cooper
ISBN: 1-903425-63-8. £9.99

Foul Deeds and Suspicious Deaths in Colchester, Patrick Denney
ISBN: 1-903425-80-8. £10.99

Foul Deeds and Suspicious Deaths in Coventry, David McGrory
ISBN: 1-903425-57-3. £9.99

Foul Deeds and Suspicious Deaths Around Derby, Kevin Turton
ISBN: 1-903425-76-X. £9.99

Foul Deeds and Suspicious Deaths in & around Durham, Maureen Anderson
ISBN: 1-903425-46-8. £9.99

Foul Deeds and Suspicious Deaths in Hampstead, Holburn & St Pancras, Mark Aston
ISBN: 1-903425-94-8. £10.99

Foul Deeds and Suspicious Deaths in Hull, David Goodman
ISBN: 1-903425-43-3. £9.99

Foul Deeds and Suspicious Deaths Around Leicester, Kevin Turton
ISBN: 1-903425-73-1. £10.99

Foul Deeds and Suspicious Deaths in London's East End, Geoffrey Howse
ISBN: 1-903425-71-9. £10.99

Foul Deeds and Suspicious Deaths in Manchester, Martin Baggoley
ISBN: 1-903425-65-4. £9.99

Foul Deeds and Suspicious Deaths in Newcastle, Maureen Anderson
ISBN: 1-903425-34-4. £9.99

Foul Deeds and Suspicious Deaths Around Newport, Terry Underwood
ISBN: 1-903425-59-X. £9.99

Foul Deeds and Suspicious Deaths in and Around Scunthorpe, Stephen Wade
ISBN: 1-903425-88-3. £9.99

More Foul Deeds and Suspicious Deaths in Wakefield, Kate Taylor
ISBN: 1-903425-48-4. £9.99

Foul Deeds and Suspicious Deaths in York, Keith Henson
ISBN: 1-903425-33-6. £9.99

Foul Deeds and Suspicious Deaths on the Yorkshire Coast, Alan Whitworth
ISBN: 1-903425-01-8. £9.99

Please contact us via any of the methods below for more information or a catalogue.
WHARNCLIFFE BOOKS
47 Church Street – Barnsley – South Yorkshire S70 2AS
Tel: 01226 734555 – 734222; Fax: 01226 724438
E-mail: enquiries@pen-and-sword.co.uk
Website: www.wharncliffebooks.co.uk

STRANGEWAYS

A CENTURY OF HANGINGS
IN MANCHESTER

MARTIN BAGGOLEY

Series Editor
Brian Elliott

Wharncliffe Books

For Rachel and Philip
who once came with me
to Strangeways

First Published in Great Britain in 2006 by
Wharncliffe Books
an imprint of
Pen and Sword Books Ltd
47 Church Street
Barnsley
South Yorkshire
S70 2AS

Copyright © Martin Baggoley 2006

ISBN: 1 903425 97 2

The right of Martin Baggoley to be identified as Author of
this Work has been asserted by him in accordance with the
Copyright, Designs and Patents Act 1988.

A CIP catalogue record for this book is available from the
British Library.

Typeset in 11/13pt Plantin by Concept, Huddersfield.

Printed and bound in England by
CPI UK.

Pen and Sword Books Ltd incorporates the Imprints of
Pen & Sword Aviation, Pen & Sword Maritime,
Pen & Sword Military, Wharncliffe Books,
Pen & Sword Select, Pen and Sword Military Classics
and Leo Cooper.

For a complete list of Pen & Sword titles please contact
PEN & SWORD BOOKS LIMITED
47 Church Street
Barnsley
South Yorkshire
S70 2AR
England
E-mail: enquiries@pen-and-sword.co.uk
Website: www.pen-and-sword.co.uk

Contents

Strangeways Gaol, shortly after it was built. Manchester Central Library

Introduction and Acknowledgements

For several centuries Lancaster was the only town in Lancashire permitted to hold assize courts. These sat twice each year and they were the venues for the trials of those charged with very serious crimes. Anyone in Lancashire facing such a trial had to be taken to Lancaster. However, in the early years of the nineteenth century, it was becoming increasingly obvious that Lancaster could not cope with the demands of an increasing crime rate in the county. Thus, in 1835, Liverpool was granted the right to hold its own assizes and, in 1864, Manchester became an assize town. Lancaster retained its assize courts until 1971, but Manchester could try serious cases and had the right to execute those convicted of murder. Between 1864 and 1867 there were several public executions outside the walls of the New Bailey Gaol, but this had been built in the eighteenth century, and needed replacing.

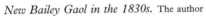

New Bailey Gaol in the 1830s. The author

An aerial view of Strangeways, showing the six wings which radiate from the centre.
Manchester Central Library

As early as 1862, Lancashire's magistrates had voted in favour of the construction of a new county gaol, despite objections that the proposed site was a densely populated area, which had once formed part of the Strangeways estate. This was behind the newly constructed Manchester Assize building. The proposal received government backing and a competition was held to find the best design. This was won by locally based architect Alfred Waterhouse, and it eventually opened in 1868, having cost £170,000. The New Bailey was demolished and the stones and bricks used in the building of the new gaol.

The Lancashire magistracy was particularly progressive, and at the meeting at which the call was made for the new county gaol, it was decided to try and have executions at that gaol carried out in private. In January 1863, five years before public executions were finally abolished, a group of them met in the Mayor's parlour at Manchester Town Hall to formulate firm proposals which were to be forwarded to the Home Secretary by local MP, Mr Hibbert. The mayor, Abe Heywood, chaired the meeting and a plan was put forward by Reverend Bagshaw. This proposed that hangings should take place within the walls of the gaol, and the only witnesses would be the High Sheriff, the governor and staff of the gaol, a special jury, and representatives of the press. These do in fact bear many similarities to the procedures which were eventually adopted, when private executions were introduced.

The Bishop of Manchester was at the meeting, and he shared some reminiscences of when he worked in London some years earlier. Every day he had to pass Ludgate Hill, and witness what he described as the 'frightfully demoralizing spectacles' of public executions, which was at a time when even forgers were hanged.

By the time the new gaol was completed on Southall Street in 1868, public executions had been abolished, and none took place outside of its walls. It was built in the Gothic style, and was effectively two gaols in one, as it held 800 men and the same number of women; and the two sexes were completely separate from one another. It was constructed using the panoptic principle, with six wings, each four storeys high, which radiated from a central point, like the spokes of a wheel. From the centre it was possible to see the whole of the gaol.

The cells were thirteen feet long, seven feet wide, and nine feet high. Each of them had tiled flooring, was well lit, well ventilated, and warm. There was a wooden bed which in the day time was transformed into a table. There was a gas jet in each cell, but the prisoner did not have control of it.

Many of the cells in the men's part of the gaol were fitted out as workshops, so prisoners could fill their time working as carpenters,

The companies involved in the building of Strangeways received a great deal of prestige locally, and this advertisement appeared in the souvenir brochure of the opening of the gaol.
The author

One of the cells in the men's part of the gaol, which was fitted out as a workshop. Manchester Central Library

weaving matting and calico, repairing and making shoes, and tailoring. The women's cells were not fitted out in these ways but they were, nevertheless, kept busy at sewing, with laundry work and keeping the building spotlessly clean by regular cleaning duties.

There was a treadmill that could be used by eighty men at one time, and this was for those prisoners sentenced to hard labour; it pumped all of the water used within the gaol from a deep well. The refractory cells were located in the basement, and it was to these that the governor sent prisoners who would not work or who broke other prison rules. They were dark and miserable, and prisoners would spend several days in one of them on a diet of bread and water.

The baths were provided with hot and cold water, and the entire building was ventilated by a system of underground tunnels connected to each cell. The system's tall minaret-like shaft, which operated as both a smoke stack and a ventilation shaft, remains a prominent feature of the Manchester skyline.

There was a large chapel, at one end of which was a private gallery for the gaol governor, other staff, and visiting dignitaries. Male and female prisoners entered through separate doors, and once inside the chapel, the sexes were divided by a large screen, which meant they could not see each other, even when at prayer. The rows of seats were on different levels, giving the appearance of an amphitheatre. The seating was partitioned into smaller sections, each of which had its own warder, sat slightly higher than the prisoners so they could all be seen.

The condemned cell was located in the basement of B wing in the men's section of the gaol. It was formed by two ordinary cells being opened up into one large cell. There were two doors, one of which led into a corridor, and the other led into the visiting area. It was here that family, friends and other visitors met with the condemned prisoner, although they were separated by iron bars, and no physical contact was allowed. This was especially so in the early years, but it does seem that this rule was relaxed later on.

To reach the place of execution, the condemned person was led out of the door and across the corridor, before passing through double doors, which opened into the execution shed which was fifteen feet square. When what was the first of the gaol's scaffolds was required, a pair of doors was thrown open, and the structure folded outwards, and was ready for almost immediate use. It was probably little comfort to the person about to be hanged that this contraption meant that the expense and inconvenience of having to erect a scaffold outside of the gaol, each time there was an execution, were avoided.

Strangeways has witnessed many changes, and it is now a male offender's institution only. In the spring of 1990, it was the scene of the country's worst ever prison riot. Severe damage was caused to the building during a twenty-five day period.

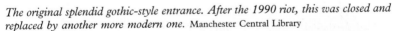

The original splendid gothic-style entrance. After the 1990 riot, this was closed and replaced by another more modern one. Manchester Central Library

When it was brought to an end, and the last of the prisoners had surrendered, extensive renovations were necessary before it could re-open. When it did accept new inmates, the government gave it the new official title of HM Prison Manchester. In abandoning the old name, it was hoped that the prison's image would be improved. To many Mancunians however, it will always be known as *Strangeways*.

The first person to have been hanged in Strangeways was Michael Johnson in 1869, and the last and one hundredth to meet his end on its gallows was Gwynne Owen Evans, in 1964. The intervening years saw four women hanged, and there were three double executions. Some of those hanged have remained notorious, whilst others have long been forgotten.

This book tells some of those stories, and I am grateful to several people for the help they have given me. Wendy Harrison has done a splendid job of typing the manuscript; S C Hunter, Geoff Parker and my wife Claire helped with the illustrations; I am indebted to Richard Seed for his drawings used in the

chapter on Buck Ruxton; staff at Bury, Rawtenstall, Rochdale and Manchester Central libraries have also been very helpful; I wish to thank the editors of the various newspapers who have allowed me to use material from their publications; and there is a special thank you to my editor, Brian Elliott for his patience and valued support.

Notices confirming that an execution and inquest had taken place were put on the main gate. Manchester Central Library

CHAPTER 1

Michael Johnson The First to Hang 1869

... in just a few minutes the pub was transformed from a scene of celebration to one of horror.

Boxing Day fell on Saturday in 1868, and that night the pubs of Salford were full of people determined to enjoy themselves. The *Cambridge Inn*, formerly known as *The Monarch*, on Regent Road, was no exception. The landlord, Richard McDermott, had hired a band so that his customers could enjoy a dance and a song. At 7 pm, nineteen-year-old Michael Johnson entered, and in just a few minutes the pub was transformed from a scene of celebration to one of horror.

Johnson, a dyer, who lived with his parents at 4 Woden Street, had been drinking and soon began to make a nuisance of himself. The young man often became aggressive and threatening after a drink, and had been causing difficulties for the landlord during the pervious week. Mr McDermott decided to eject him, as he was determined that Johnson would not spoil the enjoyment of his other customers.

As Johnson walked towards the room in which other customers were dancing, the landlord told him he must leave the pub. However, Johnson refused to do so and was threatening and abusive towards the landlord. Mr McDermott went in search of a police officer, and returned with Sergeant Toole and two constables. The sergeant approached Johnson, who was sat quietly in the taproom, drinking a glass of porter someone had bought him, and told him he must go. Johnson finished his drink and followed the police officers to the door.

'Do you think it is not a hard case to go in for a glass of ale, and not be allowed to drink it?' protested Johnson. Sergeant Toole replied that there was nothing he could do, and warned his disgruntled charge, not to re-enter the *Cambridge*. The sergeant advised him to go straight home, but sadly the young man did not follow this good advice.

Instead, Johnson returned to the *Cambridge* a few minutes later, which he entered through its back door. The unwelcome customer sat down and despite the pleas of some of his friends to allow him to stay, the landlord grabbed him, and pulled him towards the door. Johnson began to struggle, and escaped from the other man's grip, and appealed to the landlady to let him stay. However, Mrs McDermott also insisted he should leave, and the landlord managed to push him out of the door. It sprung open soon afterwards, and Johnson stood in the doorway calling Mr McDermott 'A bloody sod', whilst challenging him to a fight. Mr McDermott reached for a stick to tackle this increasingly awkward customer, but Johnson produced a knife, and made two thrusts towards the landlord.

It was at this moment that Patrick Nurney, who was standing nearby, intervened. The thirty-year-old was a fiddler with the band which was performing that night, and who lived at the *Cambridge*, where he worked as a waiter. His decision to help his employer was to have devastating consequences. He approached Johnson, saying, 'Now take a good man's advice and go away.' Johnson's reply was dismissive, for he shouted 'What the bloody hell have you to do with it?' He then lunged at Patrick, who fell backwards into the bar, with blood pouring from his thigh. He fell to the floor, exclaiming 'I am stabbed, Lord have mercy on me.' A friend, Andrew Egan, attempted to comfort the victim after Dr Wells, of nearby 90 Regent Road was called for, but he died after ten minutes, and before the doctor arrived.

It is unlikely that Johnson realized the deadly outcome of his actions, as he simply crossed to the other side of the road, and started dancing outside of the local barracks. He then went home to Woden Street, where he borrowed three halfpence from his mother to buy some tobacco. However, news must have reached him of his victim's death, and he left the area.

Superintendent Williams of the Salford police took charge of the case, and his first task was to find the suspect. Despite not finding him at Woden Street, Williams believed that the fugitive would try and make contact with his parents in the near future. He, therefore, decided to keep a discreet watch on the house himself. He did not have long to wait, for at 1 pm on Sunday, the day following the murder, the superintendent saw a boy running towards the Johnson home. Believing him to have some connection to the family, and therefore having knowledge of Johnson's whereabouts, Williams intercepted the boy before he could reach the house.

Despite not knowing the boy's identity, the experienced police officer suspected that he was acting as an intermediary between the fugitive and his family. Williams confronted him, but the youngster was not willing to divulge anything to the officer, whose powers in this situation were limited. However, he had discovered information about the boy, namely that he was a cousin of Johnson's, that his name was Ward, and that he lived in Francis Street, Hulme, close to the cavalry barracks.

Williams faced a difficult decision, for he was alone, and if he attempted to organize a raid on the house in Hulme, where he was convinced Johnson was hiding, the boy, whom he had no powers to detain, would have time to go and warn his cousin. Williams hailed a cab, and stopped to collect one colleague, before heading to Hulme. On arrival, Williams was confronted by another of Johnson's cousins, who insisted that the wanted man was not there. Nevertheless, the officers entered the house, and in one of the bedrooms Williams saw a foot protruding from under a bed. Before the officer could say anything, Johnson called out 'All right, I will come quietly. I know you have come for me.'

The two police officers found their prisoner's handkerchief, stained in blood, and as they continued the search, Johnson asked what they were looking for. On being told that it was to find the knife used in the crime, he said 'You will not find it here, and I can't tell you what I did with it.' Indeed, the search was fruitless, and the murder weapon was never found. As Johnson was led out of the house to the waiting cab, the boy Williams had seen in Woden Street, a short time earlier, came running down the street, but he had arrived too late to warn Johnson that Superintendent Williams was coming for him.

Johnson appeared at the Borough Police Court on Monday 28 December, and was remanded until the following Thursday for committal to the assizes. However, he had first to attend the inquest on Patrick Nurney, which took place on Monday afternoon at the *Duke of York* public house on Regent Road, before the coroner, Mr W S Rutter. Dr Wells described finding the victim in a large pool of blood, which flowed from a severe wound on his left thigh. Dr Wells had performed a post-mortem on 28 December, and found the wound to be two inches long and just over one inch deep. He confirmed that a knife would have caused such a wound, and that a great deal of force had been used. The victim's femoral artery had been severed, and he had bled to death as a direct result of the wound.

John Cook, who had been passing the *Cambridge* just as Johnson had been evicted, told the coroner's court that he had seen the prisoner pull a knife from his pocket, whilst shouting 'I'll hang for one of them,' before going back into the pub.

Mr Rutter told the jury that there could be little doubt that the thigh wound had been the cause of death, and furthermore, he suggested that there was no question as to who had been responsible for inflicting that wound. The only decision he believed that the jury had to make, was the offence with which Johnson should be charged. If they believed that there had been some provocation, no matter how slight, they could return a verdict of manslaughter. If, however, they believed there had been none, and that Johnson had wanted to cause a very serious injury, and death had stemmed from that, he should be tried for wilful murder.

The jury retired for just a few minutes before they returned and the foreman stated that they were unanimous in deciding that the evidence pointed to just one conclusion, which was that the prisoner had what they believed was a 'cool determination to murder' and that their verdict was one of wilful murder.

Johnson's trial took place at the newly built Manchester Assize Court, on 12 March 1869, before Mr Justice Brett. Mr Hopwood led for the prosecution and the defendant was represented by Mr Wilkinson.

The prosecution called Sergeant Toole, Richard McDermott, John Cook, Andrew Egan, Dr Wells and Superintendent Williams, all of whom combined to present a damning case against the prisoner in the dock.

Mr Wilkinson acknowledged that his client had stabbed the victim, but insisted that the appropriate charge would be that of manslaughter. He argued that there had been some provocation, as he claimed that Patrick Nurney had raised his foot to kick Johnson, and this being so, they must convict him on the lesser charge. The whole case together with Johnson's life depended on this one point.

There was no doubt that the victim had indeed raised his foot during the incident, and this was seen by several of the witnesses. Andrew Egan believed that he had attempted to kick the prisoner, and this was done in an attempt to prevent the prisoner reaching Mr McDermott, but he could not definitely say whether or not he had actually struck Johnson with his

Manchester Assize Courts. The author

foot. John Cook saw him raise his leg, but insisted that he had not kicked the prisoner. Richard McDermott, who had been standing closest to the victim, admitted that he could not state whether Patrick had raised his foot to kick the prisoner, or whether the force of the door being pushed open by Johnson, had forced his foot into the air.

The judge focused on this point in his summing up to the jury. He advised them that if they believed the victim had raised his foot with the intention of kicking the accused, or if they believed that Johnson had fallen forward after pulling out the knife, then a verdict of manslaughter could be returned. The jury took just twenty-five minutes to reach their verdict of wilful murder, but this was accompanied by a strong recommendation for mercy due to the prisoner's young age.

As the judge was placing the black cap on his head to impose the death penalty, Johnson's mother, who was sat in the public gallery, cried out, making an impassioned plea for mercy for her son. The judge made no comment, but Johnson shouted 'Don't cry mother, keep up your heart.'

The judge told the prisoner 'The crime of stabbing is a frequent crime in this city and in this district, and it would be well that many in this country should know that if a man stabs another with a knife, and a man dies in consequence, the result to him who stabs is death also.'

Following the death sentence, Johnson found himself as the first occupant of the condemned cell at Strangeways Gaol. It had been an eventful day for the young man who was also celebrating his twentieth birthday.

As Johnson sat in the condemned cell, awaiting what fate held for him, his friends and relatives organized a petition in the hope of having the death sentence commuted to one of life imprisonment. To gain support his parents wrote an open letter to all of the local newspapers, which read as follows:

Sir, – We, the parents of the youth awaiting execution in the County Gaol, Strangeways, desire by your permission, thus to offer our sincere thanks to the few friends who have already so kindly flocked to our assistance in the effort to obtain a reprieve for our unfortunate son, and should anyone feel inclined to aid us in this our last attempt, we humbly beseech them to their Christian charity, to hasten to help us, who are well-nigh weighed down by the dire calamity that has befallen our son in our old age. – I am, very respectfully yours.

It was recognised that Johnson had been raised by decent hard working and respectable parents, and their pleas for help did not go ignored. A petition, which included the signatures of the Mayor of Salford and other local dignitaries, was sent to the Home Office. The plea for clemency was based on several factors: firstly, that the jury had unanimously recommended mercy: secondly, although it had been determined that Patrick Nurney had not attempted to kick the condemned man, Johnson himself, genuinely believed at the time that it was a provocative act: thirdly they suggested that there was some doubt as to whether it had been a premeditated act: and finally they pointed to the youth of the condemned.

The execution was set for 8 am on Monday 29 March 1869, and as his fate was being decided, Johnson was in regular contact with Reverend Clarkson, the Catholic priest, and Reverend Caine, the Church of England chaplain, together with Manchester's famous prison philanthropist, Thomas Wright. Johnson spent a great deal of time reading and in prayer, and was described as being truly penitent. He also received regular visits from his distraught parents and sister.

Hopes of a reprieve were diminishing, and on the afternoon of Sunday 28 March, William Calcraft, the hangman, slipped into the gaol. It was by now clear that this was intended to be a deterrent sentence, aimed at those young men who carried knives, as indicated in the judge's comments on passing sentence. Furthermore, Johnson's statement

Attempts to gain a reprieve failed.
Manchester Evening News

THE CONDEMNED CONVICT JOHNSON.— Michael James Johnson, who now lies in the County Gaol, will be executed on Monday morning next, at eight o'clock. The order from the Crown Office was received by the governor of the gaol yesterday, and the convict was informed of it. From his demeanour he does not appear to fully realise the position in which he stands. Since his sentence he has on two occasions been visited by his mother and sisters. The scaffold will be erected in one of the interior courts of the prison, and the only witnesses of the execution will be the officers of the law and the representatives of the press.

at the time that he 'would hang for one of them', although arising from a combination of alcohol and hurt pride, pointed to the crime being a deliberate and premeditated act.

Indeed, there was to be no reprieve, and at 8 am on Monday 29 March, Michael Johnson became the first person to be executed in private in Strangeways, under the terms of the Capital Punishment Act. Despite his youth, he showed great calmness as he awaited his appointment with Calcraft. He slept well, and after breakfast, he made a special point of thanking the warders, who had been his constant companions in the condemned cell, for their kindness and support. At a few minutes before 8 am, Calcraft entered the cell, and he was greeted with a firm handshake from the condemned, before they made the short walk to the scaffold. They were accompanied by two warders, Mr Wilson the under-sheriff, Reverend Clarkson, Mr J T Hibbert, chairman of the visiting justices, and Captain T H Mitchell, the governor of the gaol.

Several members of the press were present to witness the bolt being drawn, after which the body fell through the trap. It remained rigid for a moment, but suddenly began to struggle violently for a few moments before finally becoming still and lifeless. The gaol's black flag was raised, indicating to the small crowd that had assembled outside the main gate on Southall Street, that Johnson was dead. Several of his friends were present, and shortly after seeing the black flag raised they, like everyone else, quietly left the scene.

For the first time a crowd, which included several of the condemned's friends, gathered outside of the main gate as the execution took place. Manchester Central Library

The body remained suspended for one hour, before being cut down, and being laid out for the inquest. This was held at the gaol later that day at 2 pm before Mr Rutter, the coroner. As this had been the first execution to take place in private in the city, Mr Rutter was careful to ensure that there could be no doubt as to the identity of the body laid out before the jury, and that he had been executed. The struggle to end public hangings had been a long and controversial one, and some of the more hysterical claims against private executions were that the state might not carry them out, or that the wrong person might be executed. Mr Rutter took care to ensure that there could be no such claims or any criticism about the execution or the inquest.

Captain Mitchell confirmed that Johnson had been his prisoner since 6 March, and that he had been present at the trial. The governor then produced the document authorizing the execution, and told the jury that he had been present at the execution earlier that day. Dr Braddon, the prison doctor, declared that he had also been present at the execution, and had later issued the death certificate, following a post mortem. Alexander Hayes, a warder, testified that he had been in regular contact with Johnson since his trial and during his confinement in the condemned cell. Warder Hayes had also accompanied the jury members as they inspected the body, and had identified it as that of Johnson. The jury agreed that it was Johnson's body and that he had been lawfully executed.

Afterwards, Superintendent Williams told of the journey from Hulme to Salford police office following Johnson's arrest, and the cab journey had taken them past the site of the New Bailey Gaol. As they passed, Johnson told the officer that just over twelve months earlier, in November 1867, he had been amongst the thousands who had assembled there to witness the public execution of three Fenians for the murder of a Manchester police officer. Johnson had suggested to Williams that he might meet the same end.

Since November 1867, the bodies of the Irish nationalists and the others who had been executed in front of the New Bailey were removed and reburied within the walls of Strangeways Gaol. During the afternoon of Monday 29 March 1869, Johnson was buried in a grave next to the Fenians.

CHAPTER 2

John McKenna
The Rochdale Wife-Killer
1877

The prisoner entered the dock looking pale and he was trembling.

It is difficult to imagine a more reviled individual than John McKenna when he stepped on to the scaffold at Strangeways Gaol on the morning of 27 March 1877. His crime, a murder of exceptional brutality and callousness, committed only four weeks earlier, had shocked not just the inhabitants of Rochdale, where it had occurred, but the country as a whole.

When sober, McKenna was a hard-working man, who as a plasterer could earn as much as £3 weekly in wages. However, when drunk he became extremely violent, and seemed to enjoy his reputation as a hard man. In the past this had led to several court appearances and on one occasion he was sought by the police for a serious assault at the *Freemasons Arms*. McKenna decided to leave the town, and only returned two years later, whereupon he was immediately arrested. He was brought before the magistrates, who simply fined him, as they stated that he had suffered enough, by having had to live away from Rochdale.

Twenty-six-year-old McKenna had been married to Annie, one year his junior, for six years. They had had three children, only one of whom, a three-year-old daughter, survived. Annie was known as a sober and hard-working young woman, who was devoted to her child. She worked at the local Ashworth's Mill, in Holland Street, in the card room, but had recently stopped work as she was eight months pregnant.

The marriage was marked by his violence towards Annie, and she had told her relatives, that often, after he had been drinking, she and her daughter had to seek shelter by crawling under the bed, to escape his punches and kicks. Furthermore, he had often threatened to kill her, and he had been heard by his in-laws to shout 'I will have your damned life yet.'

They had moved home several times, and in early February 1877, they rented 7 Dawson Square, a cul-de-sac, off Rope Street. It was located in a district known as The Mount, a notorious slum. Shortly after their arrival, Annie had sought shelter for three nights at the home of a neighbour and friend, Mrs Mary Higgins, who also lived in Dawson Square. However, following a promise from her husband that he would stop beating her, Annie moved back into number seven. It was to prove to be a fatal error of judgement.

At lunch time on Saturday 24 February 1877, McKenna returned home from work with his wages, some of which he handed over to Annie for her housekeeping. They then went out and met their friends, James Rushton and his wife. After visiting several pubs, the foursome returned to the McKenna home, and Annie was sent to buy two quarts of beer. McKenna, who was already very drunk from what he had consumed in the pubs, became even more so.

The Rushtons left an hour later, and as her husband was by now asleep, Annie went across to talk with her friend, Mrs Higgins. Annie told her friend that since they had become reconciled, the relationship with John had improved greatly. She praised him for being such a hard worker and for being such a good breadwinner for the family. Annie went home, but within thirty minutes, she was back at the home of Mrs Higgins, saying that John had begun hitting her for no apparent reason.

Almost immediately, McKenna could be heard outside, shouting 'I have come for my bloody wife!' Mrs Higgins told him that Annie was not there, but disbelieving her, he forced his way past her and into the house. There he found his cowering wife. He forced her out of the house, and as they crossed the square he could be heard shouting 'I'll give it to you when we get home. Will I work for such a bloody cow as you?'

McKenna pushed her through their own front door, which he slammed shut.

After a few minutes, Annie was heard to scream 'Murder!' and, concerned for her friend's safety, Mrs Higgins made her way to the McKennas' house. She peered through a gap in the curtains for about five minutes, and saw Annie being savagely beaten by her husband. Residents of The Mount did not normally call upon the police, and tried to resolve their own difficulties, and so Mrs Higgins shouted to her neighbours for assistance. Mary Ann Kelly arrived, and as Mrs Higgins went in search of Mrs Whelan, Mary kept her eyes on the scene inside the McKenna household.

For the next twenty minutes, Mary saw Annie receive a sustained and savage beating. She was kicked repeatedly besides receiving many punches to her face and body. Occasionally, McKenna would stop and sit down, as though resting, before resuming his attack. She watched as he battered Annie's head against the mantelpiece. Fearing he was about to come out into the street, Mary ran off.

It was now nine-thirty, and Mrs Higgins, together with Mrs Whelan, returned to the scene. The two women, very bravely, decided to push open the door, which was unlocked, but which was difficult to open as McKenna had placed a table across it. After a struggle, they managed to do so, and on entering the room they saw him throw a bucket of water over Annie, who by now was on her hands and knees, so as to revive her. Once he had done so, he resumed the beating. He then turned on the two unexpected visitors, who fled the scene as he walked towards them; but before leaving they had noticed that the McKennas' three-year-old daughter was in the room.

Annie was probably close to death, and it is impossible to say whether or not she might have survived had the police and medical attention been called for even at this stage. However, there would be another two visitors to the McKenna home, and whilst each attempted to help, no outside assistance was called for.

The first visitor was Henry Dunn, a work colleague of McKenna. He had called to see if his friend was going out for a drink, but was stunned to find McKenna throwing yet another bucket of water over his wife, which was immediately followed by more kicks and punches.

Henry attempted to stop the assault by grabbing hold of McKenna, who now turned against the visitor. He hurled Henry across the room, and they fell out into the street. They fought for twenty minutes, and a crowd of local residents gathered to watch them. Incredibly, even though the crowd knew about the assault on his wife, they all supported McKenna. Henry Dunn was an outsider, fighting one of their own, and instinctively, they turned against him. Fearing that they were about to attack him, Henry ran off to the home of his employer in nearby Rope Street, for shelter.

Soon afterwards, Thomas O'Day, a cousin of Annie, arrived as he had been told of the assault that was taking place. He entered the house, and saw his cousin lying on the bed in a desperate state, and clearly in great distress. McKenna turned to him and said 'We've had a bit o' bother', whereupon, he lifted Annie's head and punched her yet again in the face. Thomas grabbed him and managed to push him into a chair.

McKenna gave Thomas a shilling and told him to fetch half a gallon of ale. Hoping this might pacify him, he agreed to do so, and after he had returned, the two men sat down to drink together. He had managed to prevent further abuse, but he became increasingly concerned for his cousin, who now lay on the bed, without any sign of movement.

He approached the bed, and finding no signs of life, he said 'Why Jack she's dead.' He raised the alarm in the square, and several women arrived, but Annie was not yet dead, and had fallen onto the floor. She asked the women to bring her some water, and she was gently lifted into a chair. However, she had no control over her body, and she fell out of the chair onto the floor. The women turned to McKenna and asked him to lift her onto the bed. He stood up, and much to the horror of those present, far from helping his wife, he kicked her once more, as she lay on the floor.

Very soon afterwards, it was obvious that Annie was dead, and McKenna said he would go and fetch a doctor. However, he changed his clothes, which were covered in blood, and disappeared.

It was to be a further two hours before the police were eventually called for by Thomas O'Day. Dismayed at the delay due to the initial reluctance of the neighbours to summon the police, which meant that McKenna had a head start on them, Chief Constable Stevens initiated a massive search of the town. However, by the early hours of the morning there was no sign of him, and it was assumed that he had left Rochdale. Nevertheless, it was known that he had relatives in Liverpool, and that is where the police focused their search.

As the search for McKenna began, so did the mourning for Annie. The blood splattered walls and floor of the room, where the murder had taken place, were cleaned. The bed was moved, and a long table was brought into the room, on which Annie's body was laid out. Her mother and sister came from Heywood, and remained with the body. Her mother, Mrs Walsh, could be heard crying 'Oh Johnny McKenna, you've murdered my daughter, my poor Annie.'

The murder scene was visited by several hundred people on the Sunday, and those who came to view the body were invited to put what money they could afford on a plate that had been placed on Annie's legs. There were so many visitors that the police who had maintained a presence at the scene, had difficulty in controlling the crowd.

Annie was from an Irish family, and after the post-mortem had been performed on the Monday afternoon, at the house, her family had intended to hold a traditional wake that night. However, the police asked them to postpone it until after the inquest, which was to be held the following Tuesday.

Meanwhile, Detective Sergeant Banks, who knew the fugitive, was in Liverpool. With the assistance of the Liverpool police, searches were made of the homes of two of the fugitive's relatives, but these proved fruitless. However, letters were found at his mother's home, which showed that he had relatives in Glasgow. Sergeant Banks therefore decided to keep watch at the Clarence Dock, from where the Glasgow steamers left.

His intuition paid off, and at a few minutes before nine o'clock on Monday night, he saw his prey, making his way towards the Glasgow steamer that was about to leave. The officer placed a hand on his shoulder, and the startled McKenna could only say 'Oh good heavens' as he was led away to a Liverpool police cell, where he remained until five o'clock the following morning.

News of his arrest was telegraphed to Rochdale almost immediately, and the police decided to change their plans to take him by direct train to Rochdale, for ten o'clock. The police were worried that if a large crowd gathered to greet him, he might be attacked. It proved to be a wise decision as by nine o'clock, more than 2,000 people had gathered outside Oldham Road station.

ARREST OF THE ROCHDALE WIFE MURDERER.

M'Kenna, who so brutally murdered his wife at Rochdale, was last night arrested at the Clarence Dock, Liverpool, when about to embark for Glasgow. He was this morning removed from Liverpool to Bury, from which town he was conveyed in a police van to Rochdale. This course was adopted to avoid excitement at the latter place.

The fugitive was arrested at the Clarence Dock in Liverpool.
Manchester Evening News

The police hurriedly changed their plans, and decided to take him to Bury by train, from where he would be taken by road to Rochdale. However, news of the arrival of the Rochdale police van, drawn by its three horses, in the early hours of the morning spread rapidly throughout Bury. By nine o'clock, a large crowd had gathered at Knowsley Street station.

The train carrying the prisoner and his guards arrived at nine-thirty, and fortunately they were able to quickly make their way to the van, waiting outside of the *Knowsley Hotel*. However, members of the crowd were able to make their views about him and his crime perfectly clear, as they shouted abuse at him, and making it clear what they would do if they could lay their hands on him. The route to Rochdale was lined with many more people, and by the time the van reached Rochdale Town Hall, it was clear that if the crowd had got him, he would have been lynched.

The inquest into Annie's death was to have been held at the *Woodman Inn*, on High Street, but this was unsuitable, given the massive interest in the crime. It was therefore decided to hold it at the town hall, which could hold the many more spectators that were expected to attend.

The coroner, John Molesworth, and the jury under the chairmanship of local architect James Cheetham, entered the room first. They were followed by McKenna, who was brought up from the cells a few minutes later. He was guarded by Inspector Craig and two constables, as he sat disconsolately in the dock.

Identification of the body was provided by her mother, forty-eight-year-old Mary Walsh. She described Annie's marriage, six years earlier, and how she had lived with the couple until two weeks previously, when McKenna had thrown her out. When asked by the coroner to confirm the name and identity of her son-in-law, she shouted 'John McKenna, but he was not her husband, he was her butcher!'

Further evidence about the night of the crime, was provided by Thomas O'Day, Mary Higgins, and Henry Dunn. However, it was left to Dr Henry March, who had performed the post-mortem, to provide the most graphic evidence, to a silent courtroom. Her face was covered in bruises and scratches, and he described two large black bruises to the right side of her forehead: also her cheeks were very badly bruised: both of her lips were cut, and her lower jaw had extensive bruising. Bruises to her throat had been clearly caused by pressure being applied by thumbs, and there was a deep cut on the back of her head. There was extensive bruising to her shoulders, wrists, left hip, arms and hands. There were cuts and bruises on both of her legs.

Dr March had removed her scalp, and found her skull's surface covered in blood, and damage to the tissue which corresponded to the external injuries. He found extensive injuries throughout her body, which corresponded to the external injuries. Her lungs were slightly diseased, but all of her other organs were healthy. He confirmed that she was eight months pregnant, but remarkably, no injuries had been caused to her womb or the child.

Dr March concluded by stating that there had been no single injury responsible for her death. The injuries to the forehead confirmed that she had no doubt been concussed: scratches on her limbs confirmed that she had been dragged along the ground on more than one occasion: and all of the other injuries were consistent with her having been subjected to severe and sustained punching and kicking. The injuries to her hands showed that she had tried to defend herself, but had been unable to do so, and the assault had been prolonged. In his opinion, she had died from the accumulative effect of the beating and of shock.

At this stage, the Chief Constable stood up and advised the coroner that the police had evidence to confirm that the prisoner had threatened to kill his wife one week earlier. This had been in the presence of Annie's sister, who could prove 'malice aforethought.' He had threatened her by saying 'I will do for her in a short time'. The coroner did not think it was necessary at this stage, but no doubt the canny Chief Constable had made the point he had wished to do so in the jury's hearing.

The coroner addressed the jury, and advised them that essentially they had to decide whether McKennna should face a murder or manslaughter charge. With the chief constable's comments in mind, he stated that if an individual commits such violence towards another that death will probably follow, malice aforethought does not have to be established. He reminded the jury members that the assault was vicious and prolonged, and that there had been no suggestion of any kind of provocation.

The jury retired to the magistrates' room for five minutes, and returned with their verdict. McKenna stood in the dock with his head bowed, as he heard the inevitable verdict of wilful murder. He seemed visibly shaken, and had to support himself by leaning against the side of the dock. When asked if he had anything to say, he tried to project some blame onto Annie by saying that she had also been drunk.

He appeared before the Magistrates' Court the following day, and people started queuing several hours before the hearing was due to start. The mayor, Robert T Heape, wearing his chain of office took charge of the proceedings. The prisoner entered the dock looking pale and he was trembling. He looked unwell, as he had been refusing food since his arrival in the town on Monday. He was represented by Mr T B Ashworth.

The Chief Constable summarized the prosecution case and the witnesses who had given evidence at the coroner's court the previous day were again called. The bench was keen to establish whether or not Annie had been drunk. All of the witnesses confirmed she had not been. Dr March was adamant that she had not been drinking, and described the contents of her stomach, and the absence of any smell of alcohol. It was clear that the defence would not be able to claim that the victim had been drunk.

However, at this hearing the defence attempted to establish that Annie had been having an affair with a man named Everton. Mr Ashworth pressed Thomas O'Day about this point, presumably thinking that being her cousin he was more likely to know of this. However, he was adamant that he knew nothing of it, and he was also able to confirm that McKenna had not mentioned it on the night of the crime.

McKenna was formally committed to stand trial at the next Manchester Assizes, on a charge of wilful murder. The defence now knew that they were going to have considerable difficulty in proving any hint of provocation either because Annie had been drunk, or because of an affair with another man, and thus claiming that manslaughter was the most appropriate charge.

McKenna's trial began on Monday 5 March, little more than a week after the murder had taken place. The prosecution case was essentially that which had been presented at the inquest and committal hearing. No specific cause for the violence that night was presented, and it was argued that he was a man who did not need a reason to savagely beat his wife. The defendant's barrister, Mr Blair, attempted to persuade the jury that the charge should actually be manslaughter. He acknowledged that his client had intended to give his wife a severe beating, but if he had intended to kill her, surely, he argued, he would have used a weapon, such as the poker that was in the room at the time of the assault. He also argued that as there was no evidence to show that one specific blow had caused her death, and this also indicated that there was no intent to kill.

In his summing up the judge, Mr Justice Manisty, said that even if McKenna had not intended to commit grievous bodily harm, but death had resulted, he would still be guilty of murder. In a damning statement to the jury he observed 'I have looked at the evidence very carefully to see if there is anything at all in favour of the prisoner, and I must tell you that I did not find anything.' The jury returned their guilty verdict without retiring.

The judge then addressed the prisoner, saying:

You have been found guilty of the crime of murder, your victim being your own wife. You are a sad, sad instance of the consequences of indulging in drink, which has brought you to your present position, and it was only owing to God's mercy that it has not brought many more to the same position. If that wretched vice is indulged in as it is at the present day much longer to the extent to which it is now carried, I am afraid many more will stand in the position which you now occupy. Oh that we may put an end to this fearful vice. I hope that your case may be a warning to others.

He then sentenced McKenna to death, who was led out of the dock in tears.

The judge was not the only person to be concerned at the significant contribution alcohol had made. On 12 March, in the House of Commons, the Home Secretary was asked whether any enquiries had been made by the police into the question of McKenna being served alcohol when already in a drunken state. On that same day, the landlord of the *Albion Vaults* was charged with permitting McKenna and James Rushton to get drunk on his premises.

The issue being raised in parliament reflected widespread public concern, after James Rushton had provided details of their afternoon's drinking on the day of the murder. The men and their wives had met at the *Citizen Hotel*, after which they went to the *Drake Inn*. Afterwards they drank at the *Albion Vaults*, where McKenna paid 1s 4d for a gill of Irish whiskey, which they drank neat. He confirmed that their wives had drunk only a small amount of whiskey during the whole of the afternoon. However, the men were by now so drunk they had difficulty in standing up. James Rushton had no clear memory of subsequent events but his wife had confirmed that when they left the *Albion Vaults* at 5 pm, McKenna had fallen over almost immediately, and did so again before he reached Dawson Square.

After the trial, McKenna let his family and friends know that he wanted no visitors in the condemned cell. He attended church services regularly, and was seen by Reverend R Corbishley. No

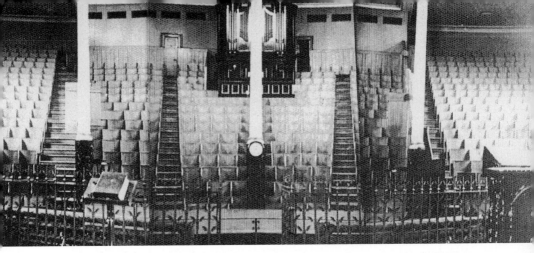

As he awaited execution, McKenna attended the chapel regularly. Manchester Central Library

petition was raised on his behalf, and no other effort made to save him from the noose.

On the eve of his execution, he went to bed at 10 pm, and spent a restless night before rising at 5 am. He was joined by Reverend Corbishley, who stayed with him until a few minutes before 8 am, when he was taken to the scaffold. He was accompanied by two warders, Mr Deacon, the acting under-sheriff, and Dr Braddon the prison doctor, together with other prison officials. Twelve journalists were gathered in the prison yard to see the procession arrive.

McKenna walked with a firm step, and stood patiently two feet away from the beam, as William Marwood, the executioner, adjusted the rope and then placed a white hood over his head. As McKenna said 'Lord Jesus have my soul', the bolt was drawn. McKenna struggled violently, swaying backwards and forwards, and he turned round several times. This struggle lasted an agonizing four minutes before the suspended body became still.

As usual, the inquest took place in the gaol at 1.30 pm, and McKenna was buried in its grounds later that afternoon, mourned by no-one.

EXECUTION
OF
JOHN M'KENNA.

THE SCENE ON THE SCAFFOLD.

This morning John M'Kenna, of Rochdale, was executed within the walls of the County Prison at Strangeways, for the murder of his wife, under circumstances of exceptional brutality, so recently as February the 24th. To say that the culprit was launched into eternity without one sympathetic word or action from any individual

The reviled murderer faced death bravely.
Manchester Evening News

CHAPTER 3

Joseph Hirst
The Body in the Canal
1896

It was immediately obvious that the baby had been the victim of foul play.

During the afternoon of Saturday 4 April 1896, a number of young lads were playing football on a piece of open land, on the corner of Cornwell Street and Ashton Old Road. Amongst them were Tommy Spicer and Frederick Worrall, who both went over to the nearby canal to clean their boots.

As they did so, they noticed a strange looking object floating close to them, which to their horror, turned out to be a baby's leg protruding from the water. With the help of their friends, they managed to lift the body out of the water, and laid it out on the towpath. The boys raised the alarm, and Constable Pointon arrived at the scene. He arranged for the body to be removed to the mortuary on Fairfield Street.

It was immediately obvious that the baby had been the victim of foul play. Around its neck were two pieces of cord which had been tied tightly, with the knot being positioned under the right ear. A piece of granite, weighing seven pounds, had been tied around its waist. Dr Heslop, the police surgeon, performed a post-mortem, and found that the corpse was that of a baby girl, aged about six months. She had been in the water for between one and four days, and the absence of water from the lungs confirmed that she was dead before being put in the canal, and that the cause of death was strangulation.

A short time before the discovery of this as yet unidentified body, a woman named Amelia Dyer, a notorious 'baby farmer', had been arrested for the murder of a number of babies, and faced trial in Reading. She had promised their parents to look after their babies for a fee, but had murdered them and kept the money. A rumour spread throughout Manchester that this was one of her victims, as there were striking similarities; she too had strangled and then put her victims in canals, and had used cord, with the knot being placed under the right ear. However, she had been in custody for some time, and had obviously been so at the time of the Manchester baby's death, so she could not possibly have been responsible for this murder.

The police did have one lead, as two women had been seen behaving suspiciously a few days earlier, and had been seen throwing some kind of bundle into the canal. They were traced very quickly by the police, who were able to confirm the women's story that they had thrown in a sack containing a cat. A search of the canal was made and the sack, together with the cat, was found. By this time, Manchester's leading police officer, Detective Chief Inspector Jerome Caminada, had been put in charge of the case, and he realised he would have to look elsewhere for the murderer.

The inquest was held on 15 April before the city's deputy coroner, Sidney Smelt, and the baby had still not been identified. After Dr Heslop's evidence, and in the absence of any progress being reported, an open verdict was recorded.

Detective Caminada arranged for the local press to be given a full description of the linen slip and skirt, and the other items of clothing found on the body, all of which were white. He hoped these details may prompt someone's memory, and fortunately they did so. Florence Chapman, a nurse, who lodged at 28 Bedford Street, Chorlton-on-Medlock, contacted him and she later identified the child's clothing and then the body. She was the baby daughter of a couple who had lodged at 28 Bedford Street but who had left just one month earlier, owing rent arrears.

Their names were Joseph Hirst, a twenty-six-year-old brick-layer, and his common-law wife, Martha Goddard, a twenty-two-year-old laundress. They had arrived at the Bedford Street lodging house on 3 December 1895, and on 10 January 1896 Goddard had been admitted to the Maternity Hospital on

The murder enquiry was led by Manchester's most famous police officer, Detective Chief Inspector Jerome Caminada. Salford Local History Library

Upper Brook Street. Fourteen days later, she had returned with their baby daughter, whom they named Maud. During their stay in Bedford Street, Florence had seen Hirst regularly beating Goddard, and had heard him shouting very loudly at Maud.

On one occasion, about a fortnight before they left, the couple had gone out, leaving Maud alone in a locked room for more than four hours. Florence had heard her crying and tried to break down the door but could not do so. She eventually got hold of a key from the landlady and took Maud to her own room, where she fed her and cared for her. When her parents returned, Florence confronted them, and threatened to contact the Society for the Prevention of Cruelty to Children, should it happen again. Hirst's response was to suggest to Goddard that she punch her.

Florence Chapman was undoubtedly a brave young woman as evidenced by her confronting Maud's parents, but had she decided to contact the relevant authorities at that time, events may have taken a different turn. Her decision not to do so simply reflected the higher level of tolerance to the ill-treatment of children at the time.

Florence was unable to tell the detective where they had gone, after leaving Bedford Street. However, the detective's colleagues, Inspectors Girdham and Watson traced them to another lodging house at 39 York Street, also in Chorlton-on-Medlock, the landlady of which was Mary French.

Mrs French remembered their arrival on 1 April 1896, as she had been concerned to see that Maud had a black eye. When she enquired about it, she was told that she had fallen out of bed. Later on that first day, Mrs French saw Goddard in the street, cradling Maud in her arms. When she asked if anything was wrong, Goddard replied 'No. It is just that I have to go out with the baby when Joe's having his tea. He doesn't like babies.'

The following day Mrs French saw the family leaving the house, and Maud was once again being carried by her mother. The couple returned several hours later, without Maud, and when asked why by Mrs French, she was told that they had taken her to Hirst's mother in Stockport, where she was being looked after. She would stay there temporarily as Martha was about to start back at work. On the following day the couple left the York Street lodging house without giving a forwarding address.

Detective Caminada visited Hirst's mother at her home in Stockport. She told him that Maud had been there a few times but she had not cared for her. Furthermore, she insisted that she did not know where her son and Maud were.

Five weeks later, a woman contacted the police to say that she knew Hirst, and that he was living at an address in Stockport. However, the police would have difficulty in recognising Hirst, as all they knew was that his most distinguishing feature was a head of bright red hair. The woman agreed to accompany the police to confirm his identity. Detective Caminada was a great believer in the use of disguise and he sent the woman to the house, with Sergeant Standen, who was disguised as a down-at-heel labourer, supposedly looking for work or hand-outs. They were followed close behind by the detective himself and several other officers, who all burst into the house when the front door opened, after Standen had knocked on it.

The woman shouted 'That's him!' whereupon, the detective and his colleagues rushed in and threw the man to the floor. However, the man did not have red hair, and as soon as he had gathered his thoughts he said 'You must be looking for my brother Joe.' The woman confirmed she had mistaken the brother for the fugitive and, following an apology, the police left, except for Sergeant Standen. Hirst's relatives still believed him to be a labouring man, and Detective Caminada made a point of shouting to his colleague to stop begging, or he would be arrested. He was invited into the house where he asked for support in prosecuting the police, and the hope was that he would be able to find out where the fugitives might be hiding. However, it appeared that his brother and his family did not know their whereabouts.

In the following weeks there were several alleged sightings of the couple; one had them staying with another brother in Nottingham; another suggested he was visiting former haunts in his home town of Derby; and another report placed him with friends in Bacup. All proved to be false leads, but eventually they were traced to a house in Leicester, and a twenty-four hour watch was kept on 43 Royal George Street by a team of police officers, led by Detective Caminada. At 1 am on Friday, 5 June 1896, the police made their move, and a startled Hirst and Martha Goddard were placed in handcuffs as they lay in bed, almost before they had woken up.

Soon after their arrest, their journey back to Manchester by train began. During the journey, Hirst discussed his predicament with Detective Sergeant Wilson and told him 'If I was to tell her to plead guilty, she would so.' The officer advised him to keep quiet until they reached Manchester, and he could have the benefit of legal representation.

Once at the Manchester Detective Office, Martha Goddard asked to make a voluntary statement. She began by telling of how she had met Hirst in Stockport in early 1895, and how they had moved from address to address in Manchester. They began living as man and wife, but he had beaten her on a regular basis, and had forced her to work as a prostitute whenever he was short of money.

She then focused on events following the birth of Maud. On 2 April they travelled to Stockport, taking Maud with them, as their landlady had said. They returned with Maud to their new lodgings at 39 York Street, and Hirst told her to fetch some fish whilst he looked after the baby. She returned to find Maud apparently asleep in her cot. She cooked the fish for Hirst, who after finishing his meal, said 'The child is dead.' At first she did not believe him, but on going to the cot and pulling back the covers, she saw that Maud was not breathing, and there were two pieces of cord pulled tightly around her neck.

He gave no reason for committing the act, but explained how he had done it; he had firstly gripped her around the throat, and then tied one piece of cord around her neck, and then the second piece. He had often told her that he wished the baby was out of the way, and although he had threatened to kill her, she had never taken the threat seriously.

Hirst then told her to wrap a shawl around Maud's body, and to go with him. They walked along Ashton Old Road and stopped on the canal towpath. He found a large piece of granite, which he tied around the baby's waist with another piece of cord, and he had then put her into the canal. The couple then made their way back to their lodgings.

Martha Goddard told Detective Caminada that she had done as she was told, as she was very much afraid of Hirst, and she was now covered in bruises and had two black eyes, following a beating at his hands.

Her written statement was read over to Hirst, who at that moment must have already begun to feel the noose tightening around his neck. He sat quietly for a few moments, and then said, 'I own to it all. I don't expect any pity. The thing is so bad. Martha Goddard is not to blame at all. She was under my influence, and did everything I told her.' Hirst then agreed to sign a copy of the statement he had just made.

The couple appeared at a special court that Saturday afternoon, and were remanded in custody until the following Thursday, when they were to be brought before Francis Headlam, the stipendiary magistrate. On that occasion they were both committed to the next Manchester Assizes, Hirst to face a wilful murder charge and Martha Goddard to face a charge of being an accessory after the fact.

On their return to Manchester Hirst and Martha Goddard appeared in front of stipendiary magistrate Francis Headlam, before their committal to the Assizes. Manchester Old and New

Their trial took place on Tuesday 14 July 1896 before Commissioner Dugdale, and the prosecution was led by Sir Joseph Leese QC MP. Mr Cottingham represented Hirst, and Mr B G Wilkinson represented his co-defendant.

The trial began with a sensational development. Martha Goddard was brought into the dock on her own, and Sir Joseph rose to address the judge. He said that she would not be prosecuted, but would be called as a witness for the prosecution. The judge agreed, and after a formal not guilty verdict was announced, she left the dock. Hirst was then brought into the dock on his own, and pleaded not guilty.

The prosecution called Florence Chapman, Mary French, and Mrs Hirst, the boys who had found the body, and Dr Heslop, who had performed the post-mortem. Mr Cottingham attempted to cast doubt on the true identity of the baby's body, and he cross-examined Florence Chapman, suggesting that she had been wrong about the baby's clothing, which he argued did not belong to Maud.

However, the most damning evidence was the statement made by Martha Goddard to the police, on their return to Manchester. This clearly incriminated Hirst in the murder, and although Mr Cottingham could not prevent her statement being read out in court for the jury to hear, he tried to prevent his client's response at the time, which was self-incriminating, and which would surely lead to his conviction if heard by the jury.

Detective Chief Inspector Caminada began to read out the woman's statement, but when he began to read out Hirst's reply, Mr Cottingham objected in the strongest possible terms. He argued that Hirst had not been represented at the time, and in support of his argument he cited three cases in which the judges had refused to allow a statement taken in similar circumstances, to be admitted as evidence. Sir Joseph countered by saying that in this particular case the statement had been read over to Hirst who, significantly, had signed it. Coincidentally, one of the judges, who had made one of the three earlier rulings, Mr Justice Cave, was at the Assizes and Commissioner Dugdale consulted him. After doing so, it was agreed that as Hirst had signed the statement it could be used in evidence.

The jury took just thirty-five minutes to return their guilty verdict, which did not include a recommendation for mercy. In sentencing him, the judge's comments suggested that there would be little hope of a reprieve. He told the prisoner 'You have been found guilty after a patient trial, and an able defence, of murdering the infant child of yourself and Martha Goddard. I do not wish to say anything to aggravate the feelings which must influence you at this moment. The only thing I do is to advise you to spend the days remaining to you in seeking the forgiveness of Almighty God.'

MURDER OF A LITTLE GIRL.

DEATH SENTENCE.

A TERRIBLE child murder case was tried at Manchester Assizes. Joseph Hirst, twenty-six, a bricklayer, and a native of Derby, was charged with the murder of his female child on April 2. Originally the mother, a laundress, named Goddard, with whom Hirst cohabited, was charged with being accessory, but that charge was abandoned, and Goddard became the principal witness for the prosecution. She described with startling detail how the prisoner, who was tired of the child, sent her out, and when she came back told her the child was dead. He told her he held it by its throat with his fingers, and then tied first one piece and then another piece of cord round its neck. Then he told her to hide the dead child under a shawl and come out with him, and during the walk he took the body and put it into the canal.

Prisoner was sentenced to death.

The case received a great deal of national publicity.
The Illustrated Police News

After being sentenced to death, Hirst accepted his fate with equanimity. He was visited regularly by his mother and brother, and Martha Goddard also visited him in the condemned cell. His mother visited him for the last time on Saturday 1 August, as the execution had been set for 8 am on the following Tuesday.

[TH]E CONDEMNED MEN IN STRANGE-WAYS GAOL.

DATE OF EXECUTION.

We learn from a reliable source that the two men, [Hir]st and Rennison, who were condemned to death at [the] recent Manchester Assizes, are in good health. Hirst [has] been visited by his mother and brother, and has [also] had an interview with the woman Goddard, who, it [will] be remembered, was indicted at the same time as [Hir]st, but acquitted, no evidence being offered against [her.] Rennison has been visited by his father.

[T]he date of execution has been fixed for next Tuesday [wee]k at eight o'clock.

There were no journalists present at the execution, but prison officials reported that the condemned man had posed no problems, and the execution, which was carried out by Billington, went ahead without a hitch. The crowd of

Hirst was not the only convicted murderer awaiting execution, but the other man was reprieved. Manchester Evening News

200, who had assembled outside of the prison gates, quickly dispersed once the traditional black flag had been raised.

At the inquest, held that same afternoon, Dr John Edwards, the gaol surgeon confirmed that Hirst's neck had been dislocated, and that death had been instantaneous. The jury returned the formal verdict that death was caused by hanging, duly carried out according to law.

CHAPTER 4

Joseph Holden
The Bury Tragedy
1900

I took him by the scruff of the neck and breeches, and threw him down the quarry.

I t was shortly before 11 pm on Wednesday 5 September 1900, that a man approached Sergeant Arrowsmith, as he walked along Railway Street, Radcliffe. The dishevelled man said to the officer 'Lock me up'.

'What for?' asked the surprised policeman.

'You will see' replied the man, as he was led away to Radcliffe Police Station.

When they arrived, the man again insisted 'Lock me up' and then said 'I have murdered a boy in Bury. I have thrown him down a stone quarry near to the *Sun Dial,* about half past five this afternoon.'

Sergeant Arrowsmith warned him that whatever he said would be written down, and could be used as evidence against him. This, however, did not deter the detained man, who continued by saying 'It is true. His name is John Dawes aged eight years, and he lives at 18 Nuttall Street, Bury, and I am grandfather to him.'

This brief statement was written down by the Sergeant, and signed by Joseph Holden, a fifty-seven-year-old former iron turner, who was locked in a cell, whilst a telephone call was made to the Bury Police Station.

This was answered by Sergeant Swainbank, who immediately recruited a number of colleagues. They made their way to the quarry at Top-o'the-Hill, which was situated off Walmersley

Road, behind Bury Infirmary, and which had not been in use for some years. They began dragging the water-filled quarry at 12.30 am, and five hours later found the body of a young boy in six feet of water. The body was immediately taken to the mortuary at the local fire station.

Details were passed to the Radcliffe police, and Holden was again questioned, and volunteered another statement. He told Sergeant Arrowsmith 'I took him by the scruff of the neck and breeches, and threw him down the quarry. I then went down into the quarry to him. He seemed to be bleeding from the back of the head. I picked him up again and threw him into the water.'

The prisoner was taken to Bury, and he arrived at the police station at 7.30 am. Sergeant Swainbank was entering Holden's details in the charge book, when the man asked the Sergeant 'Have you found his cap?'

'No' replied the Sergeant, who added 'His right clog is missing also.'

Holden continued by saying 'His clog and cap are there. I saw them come off as he was going down the quarry.'

Following this statement, a further search was made of the quarry, where a boy's cap and right clog were found among some large stones, about twenty feet from the water, where the body had been found earlier. A dozen drops of blood were also discovered, leading from the stones. It was clear to Sergeant Swainbank that the victim had been attacked initially where the stones were, and as he had been carried to the water's edge, blood had dripped from a head wound, which he had seen on the body.

Later that same morning, Holden was brought before the local magistrates, where the police case was presented by Inspector R Noblett. It had only been a few hours since John's body had been discovered and, as yet, no post-mortem had taken place. However, the police had sufficient grounds for holding him, given his confession, and the statements regarding the cap and clog, which indicated that he had been at the quarry to know as much as he did about the events there.

Furthermore, the police enquiries during the night had led them to decide that he would be charged with the attempted murder of another of his grandsons two weeks earlier. This was nine-year-old George Eldred, who had suffered a serious head wound in late August, which until now had been viewed as being the result of an accident. Holden was remanded in custody until Saturday morning, after the court had been told that a post-mortem would be completed later that day, and the inquest on John was scheduled to take place on Friday.

The inquest was held at Bury Town Hall, before the coroner, Mr S F Butcher. There were many distressing scenes throughout the duration of the hearing, and John's mother collapsed, and others who were relatives of both the accused and the victim were in tears.

The first witness to be called was Sarah Alice Dawes, the victim's mother, and daughter of the accused. She explained that she had had sole responsibility for bringing up her children after her husband had deserted them four years earlier, having emigrated to America. Since then she had taken in washing to support herself and her family. She told the court that John had gone to school on Wednesday at 1.30 pm, and had been in his usual good spirits and he was in very good health. The prisoner, who had been staying with her, had left the house earlier that morning at 9.30 am.

When asked by the coroner if he had any question to ask his daughter, Holden shouted 'I don't want to ask her any questions, but it is a damned good job she weren't there or else she would have gone down in place of the child.'

This outburst was the first indication of any motive for the crime, for it was to emerge later that he felt he had been treated very badly by his children. This resentment had apparently festered for some time, and was to find an outlet in the killing and attempted murder of his grandsons.

Further evidence about the Wednesday's events was provided by John's teachers at St Thomas's School. Jane Robinson, assistant mistress, who had taught John, told the

Holden at the inquest. The Guardian (Bury)

court that the prisoner had called at the school on Wednesday afternoon at 3.20 pm, and asked to take John out of his class. Miss Robinson went for the headmaster, Edwin Ashton, who later advised the court that when he had asked the prisoner why he wanted to take the boy, he had replied 'His mother wants him to go an errand to the *Sundial*. I cannot go myself, as I am going to Heywood.'

A member of the jury asked if the boy had gone voluntarily, to which Mr Ashton replied 'He left with a happy smile on his face, and turned and smiled as he went through the gate.' Mr Ashton confirmed that the prisoner did not seem agitated or drunk, and when asked by another jury member if the boy had ever seemed to be suicidal, the headmaster replied 'He was a happy intelligent little lad.'

The next to give evidence was Dr Arthur Nuttall, who had performed a post-mortem on John, whom he described as a healthy and well nourished lad. Dr Nuttall had found a wound to the right side of the head, from which a great deal of blood had flowed. There was a large bruise on the left side of the forehead, and another just above the right kneecap. He believed that the injuries had been caused by blows and by falling, and had occurred shortly before death. His internal examination confirmed that death had been caused by drowning.

At the close of the evidence, the coroner asked the prisoner if there was anything he wished to say. Holden replied 'What I have to say about th' job is this 'ere. What they've got they've asked for, an' have done for two or three years.'

Turning to the jury, the coroner advised them that they had to decide how they believed the youngster had met his death, and what role, if any, the prisoner had played in it. He highlighted the alleged confession and other incriminating

The Sundial. The author

statements regarding the cap and clog, which indicated that he had a great deal of knowledge about the events at the quarry.

He continued by stating that it was not appropriate at this stage to consider the prisoner's mental state, as that was a question for another court. After retiring for a few minutes the jury returned with their verdict; they found that John's death had been due to drowning, and they found that Holden was responsible for the wilful murder of his grandson.

The coroner committed him for trial to the next Manchester Assizes, and added that the jury had requested that their sympathy be extended to John's mother. He added his own, and said that he was sure that he was expressing the feelings of the whole of Bury, to which those in the courtroom responded with a loud 'Hear, hear.'

There was also a sense of disbelief in the town that such a crime could be committed, and this turned to anger, as Holden waited with his guards on the platform of Bolton Street station for a train to take him to Strangeways Gaol, where he was to be held on remand. There were a number of people glaring at him, but he continued to present an appearance of disinterest. However, a young woman, who was obviously enraged, pushed forward and shook her fist at him, screaming 'If I could get hold of you, I'd tear your liver out,' at which Holden seemed shocked and distressed and, for the first time, he showed some emotion.

Meanwhile, further evidence was gathered relating to the alleged attempted murder of George Eldred, another of the accused's grandsons. George was a keen pigeon fancier, and his grandfather had used this to lure him away from home. George's deposition was taken down before Alderman C Brierley, who acted as a witness, and it read:

I was nine years of age in February last. I remember Tuesday the 21st of August last. I saw the prisoner, my grandfather, that day in the afternoon. He asked me if I would go with him for two pigeons. I went with him to Birtle, to a quarry. He told me to sit down on a stone and I did so. He asked me to cut some tobacco for him. He gave me a knife and I cut the tobacco. Whilst doing so, a stone hit me on the back part of my head. The prisoner sent the stone at me. I saw him pick it up with both hands. My head bled and it hurt me. He tied his own handkerchief around my neck. The blood was trickling down my head. He only struck me once. The stone was as large as a football. I walked back to Walmersley Road, and then he put me on a tram, and left me. I felt ill on the tram from the pain in my head, and on getting home my father took me to Dr France. I have been in bed since a week last Tuesday. I feel ill now, and Dr France is attending me.

When George had first told his parents about what had happened they did not believe him, and put it down to being an accident. Dr France had in fact advised them to contact the police as he was suspicious and seems to have believed the lad, but they did not do so, unable to believe that his grandfather could behave in such a manner.

One is left wondering what lay at the root of this incident; was it a trial run by Holden? Did he lose his nerve on this occasion? Or was he perhaps interrupted? We will never know, but George, who made a full recovery, could count himself a very lucky lad.

The question on everyone's lips was how could a man kill his grandson, and an answer was looked for in his background. He was a local man, who as a youth had started as an apprentice with Messrs Robert Hall & Sons, at their Hope Foundry. He had spent all of his working life there, and was an iron turner by trade.

He married and he and his wife were happy together and had eleven children, all of whom survived. Five had married by the time of John's death, and the others had continued living at the old family home at 81 Ingham Street, after their father's problems had begun in 1896. Until then, all of the children described him as having been 'the best of fathers and a thoroughly respectable man.'

Unfortunately, his wife died in 1896, and afterwards he began drinking heavily as he turned to alcohol for solace. He was often drunk, and he was dismissed by his employer due to this. In August 1897 he appeared before Bury Magistrates' Court, charged initially with drunkenness. However, this was amended to 'wandering abroad whilst of unsound mind', which resulted in his being sent to the local workhouse.

Enquiries of Mr W H Bailey, master of Bury Union Workhouse, revealed that on entering the institution he was kept under constant observation. After fourteen days he was discharged having been found to be of sound mind. Since then he had been admitted on several occasions, but always as an ordinary inmate. He had caused no problems and had always performed the tasks required of him without complaint.

After their mother's death, the unmarried children had stayed at 81 Ingham Street and their father had often spent time with them. However, as their father's drinking continued and his increasingly bizarre behaviour worsened, they refused to let him into the house. He had, for instance, knocked nails into one of the walls of the old family home, hung a rope over it, and threatened to hang himself, and although this occurred on several occasions, he made no suicide bid.

Between the periods spent in the workhouse, his three married daughters shared responsibility for his care, and these were the mothers of John and George, and another daughter who lived in Patricroft, near Eccles. This arrangement continued until early 1900, when one of his younger sons enlisted in the Scottish Rifles. This led to the unmarried children leaving Ingham Street, and going to live with their married siblings.

One consequence of this was that there was now limited space in the homes of the daughters who had shared responsibility for Holden's care. He spent more and more time in the workhouse, and came out for the last time on the Monday before he killed John. His daughters, Mrs Dawes and Mrs Eldred, had come to an agreement with him, which involved the former allowing him to sleep and breakfast at her home, and the latter would provide him with his main meals during the day. Mrs Eldred's husband would not allow him to sleep in the house, having found him with prostitutes there in the past.

This arrangement would not last long. Holden had never been heard to complain about how his children had treated him, but it seemed that he had developed a sense of resentment, possibly as he found himself spending more time in the workhouse. This feeling of being abandoned by his children was to be expressed in the most horrific fashion.

There was of course a great deal of sympathy for the family, especially for Mrs Dawes and several collections were made for her. The level of sympathy was also evident on the day of her son's funeral, during the afternoon of Monday 10 September, when many thousands of people lined the route to Bury Cemetery.

John's remains were taken from the mortuary to his home in Nuttall Street that morning, where the cortège began its journey. Reverend J Williams, vicar of St Thomas's, held a brief service in the house for family and friends, before the hearse, which was followed by three coaches, left at 3.30 pm. The mourners were led by his mother, siblings and his large extended family of aunts, uncles and cousins. George was still too ill to go, but the procession passed his home on Ingham Street, and he could be seen watching from his bedroom window.

The hearse was preceded by twelve boys who had been John's playmates, each of whom carried a small bouquet of flowers. The polished oak coffin was hidden by floral tributes, which included one from the teachers and scholars of his school. At the cemetery the crowd was estimated to have been between 8,000 and 10,000 people. As John's coffin was being lowered into the grave his playmates threw their bouquets in, and overcome with emotion, his mother fainted at the graveside.

Holden's trial took place on Tuesday 13 November, before Mr Justice Darling, in a packed courtroom at the following Manchester Assizes. He was represented by Mr Gibbons, and Mr McKeand prosecuted. The defendant appeared unconcerned about the proceedings and what might happen to him. When asked to enter a plea, he replied 'Guilty.' The judge asked him if he was aware of the seriousness of the charge he faced, to which he replied 'Yes sir.' Mr Gibbons could not persuade his client to change his plea, and the judge ordered that the jury should first of all decide if Holden was able to understand the gravity of the charge, and if he was fit to plead. Several medical witnesses had been called to give evidence at the trial, but they were called before the trial proper started, to give their views on Holden's current state of mind.

Whilst he had been held at Strangeways, Holden had been kept under observation by the prison medical staff. Dr Edwards, the resident medical officer at the gaol advised the court that he had examined the prisoner on 15 September, and as far as he was concerned Holden was sane. Since then he had seen him almost daily, and he had always seemed to be able to appreciate the seriousness of his predicament. Dr Edwards was confident that he was fit to instruct council and to enter a plea.

Dr Edwards was cross examined briefly by Mr Gibbons who began by asking the witness 'Do you say that this man is perfectly sane now?'

'I think he is quite sane. I have no reason to think he cannot plead to the charge.'

C P McKeand, one of Manchester's most distinguished lawyers, prosecuted Holden at the trial. Manchester Faces and Places

'Have you observed any symptoms recently of brain disorder?'

'No, I don't know that I have. He has unequal pupils occasionally.'

'Is that a sign of a disordered brain?'

'It may or may not be,' concluded the doctor.

The evidence provided by Dr Edwards was supported fully by his deputy, Dr Smith, who had also seen the prisoner on a regular basis. Mr Gibbons then called Dr Ley, medical superintendent of the Prestwich Asylum, who confirmed he knew the prisoner, and since the crime, he had seen him in October, and shortly before the hearing was opened that morning.

However, Dr Ley's evidence was not particularly helpful to the defendant, although he did believe Holden was showing signs of mental and physical degeneration, and that he was of unsound mind, stemming from organic brain disease. Mr Gibbons asked if he believed Holden had been of sound mind when he had killed John, but at this, the judge intervened, stating 'That is not the question. The question the jury have to try now is whether or not he is in a fit state of mind to plead to this indictment.'

The judge then addressed the witness directly, and asked 'Does he know what he says when he pleads guilty?'

Dr Ley replied 'I think he is quite capable of pleading, and that he understands what he is charged with.'

Mr McKeand asked the doctor 'Is he quite capable of defending himself or of instructing his counsel?'

'I think so' was the response.

The judge turned to the jury and asked them to decide if, from the evidence they had just heard, they believed Holden was in a condition to plead and instruct his defence counsel. After a few minutes' deliberation the jury decided that he was able to do so. The charge was thus put to him again, and once more he pleaded guilty. Mr Justice Darling had no alternative than to place the black cap on his head, and address the prisoner:

Joseph Holden, you have with full knowledge of what you were doing, pleaded guilty to an indictment charging you with wilful murder. There remains only one thing for me to do. If you are not all together in such a condition of mind that the Crown will exact full penalty for the crime, which you have confessed, and which on the evidence no one could doubt you to be but guilty, then the Crown will deal with you in its mercy. My duty is simple. It is to pass sentence according to the law. It is that you be taken hence to the place of execution, and there be hanged by the neck till your body be dead, and that your body be buried within the precincts of the building in which you were confined. And may the Lord have mercy on your soul.

There can be little doubt that the judge himself believed that the issue of Holden's sanity at the time of the murder had not been resolved satisfactorily. Having been advised of these comments, the Home Secretary ordered that the prisoner continue to be monitored closely, and the question of his sanity be kept under review, whilst he was in the condemned cell.

However, it was decided that the execution should take place, and as he awaited the carrying out of the sentence, his apparent indifference gave way to remorse and grief. During this period there was also a reconciliation with many of his children, although not with the mother of John.

The execution was fixed for Tuesday 5 December at 8.00 am, and in the days preceding this he was in regular contact with the prison chaplain, Reverend C Williams. On the Saturday before the execution he was visited by Mrs Lord, his daughter, who lived in Patricroft, and his sister, Mrs Thornley. However, the most emotional meeting took place on the eve of the hanging, when he was visited by his daughter, Mrs Eldred, the mother of George. The youngster had also arrived at the gaol, and his mother had wanted him to see his grandfather, but the governor, Mr R D Cruikshank, thought it better not to let

the boy in. Nevertheless, the meeting was one of great emotional intensity. There was much weeping by those present, and the prisoner said to his daughter 'I have been a good father once Fanny,' to which she replied 'Yes you have father.' He

Holden was sentenced to death by Mr Justice Darling. The Manchester Evening Chronicle

Holden and his family photographed in happier times in 1887. Bury Times

asked her to look after his youngest son, who was just fifteen years old, and he told her that he hoped for the forgiveness of the whole family at some later time. Mr Cruikshank ended the visit ten minutes before it was due to close, as father and daughter were becoming increasingly distressed.

The following day James Billington carried out the execution, and Holden reportedly approached the scaffold with a firm step, and it passed off without incident. The prison chaplain later reported that Holden had told him that the murder was committed to avenge the perceived wrongs by his children following the death of his wife.

The feeling remains however, that the matter of his sanity at the time of the crime, was not fully investigated. The question remains as to whether a sane man would murder a child he loved, because of what he viewed to be the failings of the victim's mother. This scenario becomes even more difficult to understand when it is remembered that she was one of only two or three of his several children who continued to support him.

Following the inquest, which was held as usual a few hours after what was the thirtieth execution in Strangeways, Joseph Holden was buried within its walls, the only person who was to hang in the United Kingdom in the twentieth century for the murder of a grandson.

CHAPTER 5

John Griffiths
The Shaw Outrage
1906

... Kate's distraught mother and sister arrived at the inquest, each of whom was wearing a black shawl.

At 8 pm on Tuesday 19 December 1905, Kate Garrity, an attractive and popular seventeen-year-old girl, left the family home at 12 Middle Street, Mossley, in Shaw near Oldham. She went to fetch her parents a jug of beer and some whisky, to have with their supper. Her little brother asked if he could go with her and buy some chips. However the chip shop would not be open for another thirty minutes, and so she decided to go to *The Blue Bell*, on Market Street first, but promised him she would go and buy him some chips later. She was in good spirits and was singing to herself as she picked up a quart jug and noggin bottle, together with a two shilling piece, which her mother handed her.

Her parents became extremely worried when she had not returned one hour later. Her father, John, made several searches of the area during the next few hours. He later went to the Shaw Police Station to voice his concerns. The officers on duty suggested he should wait until the following morning, by which time she would probably have arrived home safely.

The Garrity family passed an anxious night as they waited for Kate to come

Kate Garrity. The Standard (Oldham)

home. She had not done so by 7 am, and John returned to the police station. On his arrival he was given the devastating news that the body of a girl had been discovered one hour earlier. It was quickly established that it was indeed the body of his daughter.

The body had been discovered by Robert Griffiths, who stabled a pony on Green Lane. At 6 am, he was making his way along the track leading to his stable, to feed his pony. As he walked along the narrow lane he noticed some sacks, but thought little more about them. When he reached his stable, he found that his sacks, which contained oats for his pony, were missing. He retraced his steps to see whether the pile of sacks he had just seen were his. As he approached them, he noticed

Kate's body was discovered by Robert Griffiths. The Illustrated Police News

No. 2185. [REGISTERED AT THE G.P.O. AS A NEWSPAPER.] **SATURDAY, DECEMBER 30, 1905.** Price One Penny.

THE ACCUSED FAINTS IN THE DOCK.

DISCOVERY OF THE GIRL'S BODY.

MYSTERIOUS DEATH OF A LANCASHIRE GIRL.
HER DEAD BODY FOUND NEAR OLDHAM.

a pair of clogs sticking out. Thinking it was probably a man sleeping off the previous night's beer, he gave them a kick. There was no response and so he pulled the sacks back; there he did not find a man sleeping off a hangover, but the body of Kate Garrity.

The shocked and distressed man immediately went to Shaw Police Station, where he was met by Constable Moffatt. On hearing the man's story, he went immediately to the scene, before calling Dr Kinnear, the police surgeon. The body was taken to the nearby *Duke of York*, where he conducted a preliminary examination. He discovered marks on her neck, which indicated that she had been strangled. The coroner was therefore informed and the police began a murder investigation.

Meanwhile, news of Kate's death had spread around the neighbourhood. Her boss at the Lyon Mill, William Turner, described her as an excellent worker, who was always willing to help others, and he said that she would be missed greatly by her saddened workmates. Mrs Johnson, the next door neighbour of the Garrity family spoke highly of Kate, whom she had known since she was child, and who was a favourite in the now deeply saddened surrounding streets. A visibly upset Father Burke of St Joseph's Catholic Church spoke of a devout, helpful and respectable girl, from a good and decent family, who would be missed greatly by him and the other church members. He no doubt reflected the views of the whole of the district when he said her death would cast a gloom over the forthcoming Christmas festivities.

Having spoken with Kate's family the police quickly focused their attention on a local youth, nineteen-year-old John Griffiths, son of the man who had discovered the body. The teenagers had been courting for several months, before Kate had ended their relationship in November 1905, since when her former boyfriend had been harassing her.

Griffiths had written to Kate on several occasions, seeking to resume his relationship with her, but she had refused to do so. In November he had seen her talking to another young man named John Newall, whom Griffiths punched to the ground, screaming 'I'll knock your bloody nose off'.

Lyon Mill. Claire Baggoley

On 3 December, a little over a fortnight before the murder, there was a further serious incident. Kate was with a friend, Elizabeth Ann Robinson, when Griffiths approached the girls, demanding to know what they were doing. He did not believe Kate when she said she was going home, and an argument followed. It grew more intense and louder, which attracted a crowd of almost 100. Constable Moffatt arrived at the scene, where he found Griffiths refusing to let Kate pass and make her way home, before slapping her across the face. As a result of this, Griffiths appeared before Royton Police Court on 13 December, where he was bound over to keep the peace for three months.

Later, his workmate, John Bardsley, asked Griffiths what had happened, to which he replied 'I asked her to go for a walk but she would not do so, and I only gave her a love tap'. The day following the court appearance, Griffiths asked his friend if he would ask Kate on his behalf to meet him after work. Upon hearing that she had refused to do so, he said 'I will do for her before Christmas'. John told Kate of his threatening reply to which she said 'He will get three months if he starts bothering me again'.

Griffiths. The Standard (Oldham)

The police thus had a suspect, who had refused to accept that his relationship with the dead girl was over; who had assaulted a man she was seen talking to; who had assaulted her, and been taken to court; and who had been heard to threaten her, having been told she would not meet with him. Having established jealousy and revenge as probable motives for the crime, the police began to build their case against him.

They traced several witnesses who had seen Griffiths on the night of the murder from about 7.30 pm onwards. Some had seen him alone, and others had seen Kate. However, none of the witnesses could positively state that he or she had seen the couple together.

At about 7.50 pm, a group of young men, Thomas White, Arthur Sutcliffe, Joe Garside, William O'Connor, and the suspect's brother, Charles Griffiths, came across Griffiths outside of the *Duke of York*. They talked together for about thirty minutes, before Griffiths left the others, saying that he was going home, as he was hungry. It was whilst walking home that the chance meeting with Kate occurred, close to where his father kept his pony, as she would also pass this spot on her way to buy the beer and whisky. They met before Kate reached *The Blue Bell*, as the landlord, John Lord, told the police that the girl often called in for beer and whisky for her parents, but she had not done so on the night of the murder; he also confirmed that her father had called at the pub at 9.30 pm looking for her.

James Taylor of Leach Street, near to the murder scene, was standing in his doorway between 8.30 and 9 pm. He saw a young man dragging a young woman in the direction of the narrow path leading to the stable, but he could not identify either of them. Marion Morrissey and Clementine Leach passed the scene, where they met with Kate who was on her own, and this must have been just a few moments before Griffiths came along. Mark Sanderson saw a young couple at the spot at the relevant time, and although he could not identify either of them, he heard a scuffle after he had passed them. He turned around to hear the girl say 'No don't, or I shall shout', whereupon the young man released his grip as he had been trying to drag her down the narrow lane where Kate's body was subsequently found.

Despite the shortcomings of these witness statements, the police considered there to be sufficient circumstantial evidence to suggest that there had been a chance meeting of the couple, as he made his way home and as she was walking to *The Blue Bell*, and this had resulted in the murder being committed.

The police also discovered from members of the Shaw Temperance Hall, that Griffiths, who played football for the club's team, had entered the premises at 9.30 pm, following the murder, and had gone to the snooker room.

Physical evidence was found at the scene of the crime that incriminated Griffiths. Kate had been strangled but she had put up a fierce struggle, which meant there were traces of blood at the scene and also on the suspect's coat and shirt. These were sent to the County Analyst in Liverpool, where Griffith's clothes were examined by William Roberts, who could only confirm that the blood was mammalian and that it had been shed recently.

However, by far the most damning piece of physical evidence was that discovered on Griffith's clogs, or rather his mother's clogs, as he had borrowed them on the night of the crime. He borrowed his mother's clogs frequently, as he did not have any of his own at that time. The right clog had a piece of iron missing from the sole, and left a distinctive imprint. As the murderer left, having covered the body with sacks, he had stepped into some ultramarine paint, spilt earlier by a local painter, whose yard was close by. This left a trail, which led from close to the body, for more than 100 yards, and which ended near to Griffith's home. The police made casts of the clog imprints and when compared with his mother's there was a perfect match.

Griffiths was arrested on Thursday 21 December, and was formally charged with Kate's murder. Meanwhile, the murder scene was being visited by many hundreds of local residents and some from much further away. A local reporter came across one of Kate's distressed friends at the scene who described her murder as 'A cruel, dastardly outrage'.

There were also several hundred people packed in the streets surrounding Shaw Town Hall, where the inquest was held, on the morning following the murder. They witnessed a pale and distressed prisoner alighting from the cab which had brought him from the police station. At 10.30 am, Kate's distraught mother and sister arrived at the inquest, each of whom was wearing a black shawl. Several times, Mrs Garrity was heard to cry out 'Oh my dear child'.

The inquest opened before the coroner Mr F A Molesworth, and local pawnbroker, John Maiden was chosen to act as foreman of the jury. Before any evidence was heard, the coroner and jury made their way to the *Duke of York*, to view Kate's body where it still lay, before going on to the scene of the crime.

At the resumed hearing formal identification was provided by Mrs Garrity, and she confirmed that Kate had only two shillings on her at the time of the murder, and that her life had been insured for just £13, and her parents were the beneficiaries. This information served to demonstrate that neither robbery by an unknown person, nor financial gain for the family, were motives for the murder. Finally, he asked Mrs Garrity if she had anything else she wished to say. She did and pointing to the prisoner in the dock, she cried out 'No nothing, unless that she was in dread of her life going out from the fellow.' Griffiths shouted 'Why should the witness tell a lie. I never had anything against the girl. I did not see her that night, only coming from my work.'

Dr Kinnear told the hearing that he had arrived at the scene at 7.30 am on the previous day, and with the aid of lantern light, made his initial examination of the body there. She was lying on her back, her hands folded over her chest; her feet were together, with her toes pointing outwards; her face was swollen, her eyes protruded, and blood trickled from her nose and mouth. There were several scratches in the area between her chin and shoulders, the most noticeable of which were on her right side. There was also a mark around her neck.

The post-mortem was carried out in the *Duke of York*, at about 12 noon. All of her internal organs were healthy, and she was a well nourished and healthy young woman. Her stomach contained a few beans. Her limbs were stiff but still retained some warmth, which led him to estimate the time of death as having taken place between four and twelve hours earlier. The cause of death was strangulation, and the markings on her neck confirmed that it had been done with a thin piece of cord. The scratches had been caused by a pin in the victim's shawl.

Dr Kinnear ruled out suicide and said that there were no signs of violence to her private parts, so she had not been the victim of a sexual assault. A thin piece of cord had been found on the prisoner, and the doctor confirmed that it could well have been used to strangle Kate.

The coroner's jury took just ten minutes to find that Kate had been murdered but, to the astonishment of the court, had found that it had been done by a person or persons unknown. Nevertheless, Griffiths was remanded in custody, to await trial at the next Manchester Assizes.

MYSTERIOUS DEATH OF A LANCASHIRE GIRL.

◆

HER DEAD BODY FOUND IN A STABLE NEAR OLDHAM.

[SUBJECT OF ILLUSTRATION.]

THE murder by strangulation of a mill-girl at Shaw, a Lancashire village between Rochdale and Oldham, has thrown the quiet community into a state of great excitement.

The victim is a girl of seventeen, named Kate Garratty, and her sweetheart, John Griffiths, the son of the man who discovered the girl's body on lonely waste land behind some factories, stands charged with her murder. Before being remanded he fainted in the dock.

The girl was sent for some beer on the 19th instant, and did not return. On the following morning, when Griffiths's father, who is a stableman, went to bait his horses, he found the girl's body under some sacks in the stable-yard.

A verdict of " Wilful murder against some person or persons unknown " was returned at the inquest on Friday.

Later on Friday night, after the inquest had been completed, Kate's body was removed from the pub where it had been since its discovery, and taken home. There she was placed in an open plain oak coffin. The coffin bore an inscription which read, 'Kate Garrity died December 19th 1905 in her 18th year' and it was put in the parlour. The door to the family home was kept open all night, and many came to pay their respects to this popular girl. In line with local tradition, the curtains of the surrounding houses were drawn shut, out of respect.

At midday on Saturday, there was an especially touching moment when

To the surprise of everyone, the coroner's jury returned with a verdict of wilful murder by a person or persons unknown. The Illustrated Police News

Mrs Griffiths, mother of the accused, entered the Garrity home. She was sobbing uncontrollably, as she placed a bunch of holly at Kate's feet. This was just one of several floral tributes, and those made of holly, mistletoe and chrysanthemums were the most popular. There was a beautiful wreath from her friends at the Lyon Mill.

At a few minutes before 2 pm, sixty members of the congregation of her church arrived outside of the house and sang *Oh God of Mercy, have compassion*. As they sang, Mrs Garrity could be heard crying above their voices 'Oh my poor Kate, my poor girl, she rests with God'. She broke down completely as the coffin lid was being screwed on a short time later, and fainted. However, she rallied as the hearse and four horse drawn carriages arrived, and she took her place in the first with her husband and four children. It was to be one of the last occasions upon which Kate's father would be seen, as he died a few days later, due many believed, to a broken heart.

The cortège travelled eight miles to Moston Cemetery, and in some places the crowds on the pavements were six and seven deep. Eventually, the cemetery was reached, and the coffin was lowered into the grave. Once again, a distraught Mrs Garrity fainted.

A few days after the funeral there was a surprising development in the case. Kate's mother received an anonymous letter, which had been posted at Ashford in Kent, at 11.15 pm on Christmas Day, when Griffiths was on remand, which read as follows:

Poor Kate – she was the pride of my heart, but now she's gone I can't help her. We had a few words together when she went to fetch the supper beer and I went done it for her. She didn't utter a noise, only said 'Don't do it Jack'. God help me for what I have done. I am an innocent man. I didn't know what to do with her body so I got some old sacks from off a wall and laid over it. 'God bless her' I said when I left her. She's gone. I waited to see if I could see anything concerning the murder in the papers, and I saw it in The People on Sunday, that they had accused my old pal John Griffiths over it. By the time you get this I might be miles away. I am spending Christmas at my mother's house in the best of spirit.

I suppose I shall have to swing it when I am caught. Cheer up John G God bless you. They always get the wrong men for anything of that sort.

Wishing you a happy new year. As for Kate she is gone. S H B

The letter led to a serious deterioration in Mrs Garrity's emotional state, but she handed it to the police to help in their enquiries. The police doubted that it was from the actual murderer, as they were convinced they had their man. Nevertheless they handed a copy to Griffiths' solicitor, J H Butterworth, who arranged for it to be published in the local press. Its publication led to speculation that it had been written by one of a group of gypsies, who had been camped in Shaw at the time of the murder, but who had left on 20 December. Kate had been seen speaking to one of them on one occasion, but the police described the gypsies as a respectable family group, who had been celebrating a wedding on the day of the murder. Nothing came of the letter, and as far as the police were concerned it was simply another example of a mischievous false confession, that was common in murder cases, especially those that received national publicity as this case had.

The trial of John Griffiths took place at the Manchester Assizes on Monday 5 February 1906, before Mr Justice Grantham. Mr Langdon KC led for the prosecution, and Mr W H Shawcross defended the accused man.

Mr Langdon began by telling the jury that the prosecution case relied largely on circumstantial evidence. The case was built on the evidence of the witnesses at the inquest and committal hearings who would confirm details of the nature of the couple's relationship, and his attitude after it ended. The jury would also hear evidence of his court appearance following the assault, and the threats he had been heard to make. Although it was not necessary to provide any evidence as to the motive for the murder, the crown suggested that the assault of the man he saw talking to Kate suggested that he was extremely jealous and that he also decided to take his revenge as she had ended their relationship, and refused to see him afterwards.

He acknowledged that no witness could positively identify both the victim and accused together at the murder scene on the night in question. However, he was certain that they would find the evidence conclusive that they had met, albeit by chance. He went through the timings of the movements of both youngsters, she from her home on her way to buy beer and whisky for her parents, and he after leaving his brother and friends to go home for a meal. Their separate paths had led to the scene of his assault on her, and where he had hidden the body, before going on to the Temperance Hall.

The jury were then told of the clog prints, which had been smeared with ultramarine paint, and which had left such distinctive marks leading from the body to close to the accused's home. Although the blood evidence was inconclusive, it was, the crown contended, powerful supporting evidence of their case.

After hearing the details of the post-mortem and confirmation that strangulation was the means by which Kate was killed, the crown advised the jury that a manslaughter conviction was not appropriate and murder was the only acceptable charge.

The defence had called no evidence of their own or witnesses, and relied on trying to undermine the prosecution witnesses under cross examination. Mr Shawcross suggested that all of the witnesses who said they had seen Griffiths that night had simply got the times wrong, and that it was in fact later; this meant that Griffiths could provide alibis at the Temperance Hall if the jury accepted there was some doubt. The defence also challenged the post-mortem evidence, and suggested that Dr Kinnear had got the possible timings wrong; they suggested that death might not have occurred until after 10 pm, by which time their client was in the Temperance Hall and in the clear.

The judge's summing up lasted for thirty-five minutes, and he confirmed that murder was the only acceptable verdict. He pointed out that suicide and accidental death had been rightly discounted. He told the jury that in his opinion robbery and sexual gratification were not motives, and he also told them that the anonymous letter posted on Christmas Day in Kent was 'rubbish', and should be discounted.

The jury took thirty minutes to reach their verdict and convict Griffiths, but they made a strong recommendation for mercy due to his youth. As the black cap was placed on the judge's head, the prisoner was asked if he had anything to say. He replied 'Yes sir, I have not done it. I am innocent.'

In sentencing him, the judge remarked that he agreed fully with the verdict, but such had been the nature of the crime, Griffiths should not build his hopes up of a reprieve. As he was being taken from the dock, he turned to one of the prison warders and said in his distinctive Oldham accent 'I've nobbut once to dee', but it was heard throughout the courtroom and was published in several press accounts. Whatever his intention was in saying this, it was taken by most observers to demonstrate his lack of remorse and his callous nature.

One of those sitting in the court who heard these remarks was John Ellis, who would later become one of the country's most famous hangmen. He had never been to a murder trial before, and he had decided to attend this particular one, as it took place near to where he lived, and he realised that if Griffiths was to hang, he would probably be called to act as Henry Pierrepoint's assistant. Ellis was convinced that the uttering of these few words on leaving the dock would mean there would be no reprieve for Griffiths.

In Shaw there was naturally, a great deal of sympathy for the Garrity family, and also for the parents of John Griffiths, and much to her credit, this was also expressed for the murderer's family by Mrs Garrity. The condemned was not yet out of his teens, and some locals felt that he should therefore be reprieved. However, the dilemma facing them was evident in a letter from a local vicar to the press, which read:

Dear Sir,

Perhaps you can lend me the aid of your paper to find out how public opinion in Shaw regards the possibility of a memorial to the Home Secretary on behalf of John Griffiths, asking that the jury's recommendation to mercy may be followed. I have been approached and asked to move in the matter, and it does seem to me that three things are to be said in favour of such a course; i) the youth of the condemned lad, ii) his home surroundings and lack of chance; iii) the maniacal character of the temper which led him to do the crime. On the other hand there is the utterly abominable callousness, the need of a striking example to others, and the justice of the verdict. I gather that public opinion is not in favour of such a memorial, and therefore see no use in moving. But I should be very glad to have the advice and help of any who think differently.

Yours very truly

James W Pinniger

Shaw Vicarage, Oldham, February 9th 1906

Despite his misgivings, the vicar received some positive feedback, and so an attempt was made to save Griffiths' life.

One of the first to sign the petition for a reprieve was a member of the jury that had convicted Griffiths. The juror told the vicar that the jury members had been unanimous in recommending mercy for the condemned youth. This reflected the views of many, as over the following days the vicar gathered more than 11,500 signatures. Many of these were from the local area, as although they had been shocked at the murder of Kate, they recognised that the killer was a youth, and possibly deserved mercy.

There were even hopes of a retrial when an old school friend of the condemned, Private Samuel Taylor of the 2nd Battalion King's Own Royal Lancaster Regiment, claimed to be able to provide an alibi that would clear Griffiths. Although Griffiths had mentioned meeting this friend on the night of the murder, it had not been pursued by the police or even the defence team. The soldier had returned to his home town as he was in the area to arrest a deserter, and whilst there he had met Griffiths. However, further enquiries showed that although the meeting had taken place, it had been outside of the relevant time frame, and was not helpful to the defence.

A few days before the execution was due to take place, his solicitor, Mr Butterworth, received another anonymous letter, which was signed by 'A Professional Nurse'. The letter writer claimed to know the true identity of the killer. However, this letter was dismissed as Griffiths had already written to his parents confessing his guilt. The letter dated 15 February, is a classic example of a murderer coming to terms with what he did, and confessing in the hope of helping his loved ones. He wrote:

Dear Mother and Father,

I write these few lines hoping to find you in good health as it leaves me at present. Dear mother, I am very sorry to tell you that it was me that murdered my poor Kate, mother, and it is no use but I can't keep it in any longer, and my dear mother I hope that you are not vexed at me for not telling you I did it when you came to see me, and dear mother I hope you will keep the photo of poor Kate for my sake. Dear mother, you might go and see Mrs Garrity and tell her from me that I am very sorry for what I have done and I hope that she will forgive me. Whatever caused me to do it I can't say. Dear mother you told me some friends were coming to see me but I would rather they did not come. Dear mother, tell Johnny Wright what I told him in my letter was not right and I hope he will forgive me, and ask him to burn the letter. Dear mother, I ought to have told you yesterday when you asked me, but after you had gone I was very sorry I did not tell you the truth, but I know you will all forgive me. I hope you and all will bear up and try to forget as it's none of your faults and none of you are to blame for what I have done. Dear mother, give my love to my brothers and sisters and tell them I hope none of you will be bad friends with the Garritys for my sake. Remember me to all inquiring friends and don't forget to remember me to all the Winterburn family, and dear mother, I hope that you will have that medal of mine made into a brooch. Dear mother, I am glad to say that I am a lot better off since I admitted that I have done so.

I think that this is all for now – from your unfortunate son.

John Griffiths

On 24 February the Home Secretary confirmed that there would be no reprieve, and three days later at 8 am Henry Pierrepoint, assisted as he had predicted, by John Ellis, hanged John Griffiths, who showed great fortitude on the scaffold.

The staff of the gaol in the early years of the twentieth century. It was from amongst these that warders were asked to volunteer to be with the condemned man or woman awaiting execution. The author

After the body was cut down the inquest was held, after which he was placed in a pauper's 'penny coffin'. He was buried amongst the growing number of those who had been hanged at the gaol, and laid to rest in what was known as the 'murderers' cemetery'.

More than twenty years after he was hanged, the case was used as an example of the alleged futility of capital punishment. The C W Daniel Company

THE STATE MURDER OF
JOHN GRIFFITHS & THE
ILFORD EXECUTIONS
OR
CAPITAL PUNISHMENT
CONDEMNED
An Appeal to Humanity and to the Churches

BY

H. BODELL SMITH

LONDON : THE C. W. DANIEL COMPANY
Graham House, Tudor Street, E.C.4

CHAPTER 6

Walter Martyn and John Tarkenter A Double Hanging 1911

Double executions were becoming rare events, and this may explain why for the first time ever, the High Sheriff of the county, Sir George Pilkington, attended in person.

Walter Martyn, a twenty-three-year-old barman, and twenty-five-year-old Edith Griffiths, who worked in the Eastwood's cotton waste works, had been courting for several months, when, in early September 1911, Edith arranged for Walter to live in her family home. Her boyfriend moved into 113 Adelaide Street, Heywood, near Rochdale, with Edith, her step-mother, and family. He paid two shillings each week rent and slept on the sofa downstairs, but the arrangements seemed to suit everyone. Mrs Griffiths was the widow of Edith's father, Thomas, who had worked on the railways, and the two women were very close.

Walter was well known for his even temper, but Edith had a reputation for losing hers for the slightest of reasons. She had been engaged to another man in the past, and had had a child, but that relationship had ended two years earlier. Martyn was aware of these facts, but he was not particularly concerned and was happy to assume paternal responsibility for her child.

At 8 pm on Thursday 28 September 1911, the couple left the house, saying they were going for a walk. Edith told her mother that they would be back within the hour, but by 2 am in the early hours of the following morning, they had still not returned home.

The couple had gone to Plumpton Wood, a spot popular with local courting couples, such as Walter and Edith. He later emerged from the wood on his own, and first of all went for a drink at the *Brown Cow Hotel*, where he arrived at 10.15 pm. He later called in at the *Black Bull Inn*, where he was employed, and he arrived at a few minutes to 11 pm.

He asked his employer, the landlord Richard Ramsbottom, for a tot of rum. They chatted for a few minutes before Martyn said to him 'You will need to get a fresh mopper-up in the morning.' At first the landlord assumed his employee was giving in his notice, but Martyn continued by saying 'It is through that girl'. He eventually told the landlord that Edith was dead, and that he had left her in the wood.

Mr Ramsbottom urged Martyn to return to the wood as Edith might still be alive, but in need of medical assistance. Martyn agreed to do so and left the public house. As he did so, he met Constable Arthur Taylor who, having listened to Martyn's story, escorted him to the police station, where he was questioned by Sergeant Barley. A few minutes later, the sergeant and Mr Ramsbottom, who had also come to the police station, went to Plumpton Wood, and at a few minutes after midnight, they found Edith's body.

She lay in a spot near to the River Roche, which was already infamous locally, as two people had drowned there two years earlier. Edith, who was not yet cold, was lying with her head towards the river, about fifteen yards from the footpath, and her shawl was wrapped neatly around her. A double-knotted handkerchief was tied tightly around her neck. The two men did not wait for a medical examination to be carried out at the scene, and carried the body to the local mortuary. This was after they had examined the area, and during their search they found evidence of a struggle on the nearby cinder path. A small piece of a tie, similar to that being worn by Martyn was found at the scene together with a piece of handkerchief. Later, when Martyn's clothing was examined, soil and cinders similar to that at the murder scene were found.

At the police station, Martyn gave the first of what would be eventually three different accounts of what occurred that night. Initially he stated that Edith asked him for a penny with which to buy some toffee from a shop they passed. However, she gave him the slip and after searching for her for several minutes, he found her with another man in the wood. He challenged the couple, and the other man punched him in the chest before running way. Martyn claimed not to remember what happened next, but subsequently found himself looking down at Edith's body. He told police that he did not know the man's name but he recognised him as someone who had worked at a local farm, picking potatoes, four years earlier. No such individual was ever traced, despite police attempts to do so. The police also visited the shop mentioned by Martyn, and discovered that Edith had indeed visited the premises. This however, had been at 7 pm, when she had returned two empty bottles and she had not purchased anything.

At the coroner's court, held on the following Saturday, it was established by members of the victim's family that the handkerchief used to strangle Edith was that which had been used four years earlier to cover her father's face after he had died. It was easily recognizable due to a distinct tear, and had been given to one of Edith's cousins after the burial. That cousin testified that he had lent it to Martyn a few days before Edith's murder. This was after Edith had remonstrated with Martyn about his own very dirty handkerchief.

Medical evidence was presented by Dr H F Jeffrey, the police surgeon, who testified that the victim's clothing was not disarranged, and there was no evidence of a sexual motive for the crime. Her face was swollen and dark coloured, especially her lips; and her eyes were protruding. There was a great deal of froth around her mouth and nose. The handkerchief was tied with a double-granny knot, and had been fastened extremely tightly, which had resulted in a deep wound to the neck. There was no doubt that she had been strangled.

A member of the coroner's jury had earlier asked Edith's mother if she had ever heard Martyn threaten her daughter. She replied that she had not, but Edith had told her that despite his calm demeanour, he was very jealous. The jury retired briefly before returning with their verdict that Edith had been murdered and the method was strangulation, and that Martyn was the murderer. He was thus committed to stand trial at the next Manchester Assizes.

Meanwhile, several thousand people visited the murder scene. On the Sunday following the crime, it was estimated that as many as 2,000 people were in the wood at any one time throughout the day.

All of these events proved too much for Martyn's father, John, who collapsed and died on hearing that his son had been charged with Edith's murder. John Martyn had been a coach builder and prominent figure in Heywood for many years. He had strong connections with the local church and Sunday School, and had been an active member of the Heywood Cycling Club. He was a well respected man throughout the district and, despite the accusations against his son, there was a great deal of sympathy for the Martyn family when news of John's death spread.

Edith's funeral was witnessed by several thousand people who lined the streets as the cortège headed for Heywood Cemetery, but it was marred by a Littleborough woman having her handbag and its contents of £3 stolen near to the grave-side. John Martyn's funeral was a much quieter affair, and had taken place earlier at the cemetery in St Helens, his home town. He was buried next to his wife, who had died six years earlier.

Whilst he was still being held at the local police station, Martyn asked to make another statement, in which he gave Inspector Carr another version of events on the night of Edith's murder. He now stated that they had argued, as he told her he was thinking of giving up his job at the *Black Bull Inn*, to seek more well paid work in Manchester. Edith was furious and threatened to find another man if he did so. At this he lost his temper, and grabbed her by the throat. After holding her so for just a very short time, she became quite still. He called out her name but there was no reply. In a panic, he attempted to put the tie around her neck, but it snapped, so he then used his handkerchief, for reasons he elaborated on at his trial.

His trial took place before Justice Avory on 21 November 1911. The prosecution was led by Roe Rycroft, and Mr Openshaw represented the accused man. During his evidence at the trial Martyn provided a third version of what occurred on the night of the crime.

He stated that they had gone to Plumpton Wood in order to have sexual intercourse. He insisted he had not said this at first as he wanted to protect her reputation. Once in the wood, she had accused him of having an affair with another woman. He continued by saying:

She was laughing and crying together. She was very excited. I got hold of her but did not know what I was doing. Honestly speaking I was excited – upset about what she was accusing me of. I did it to frighten her.

There was no struggle, and when he realised she was dead, he put the handkerchief around her neck, after failing with his tie, as he somehow believed this might persuade people that she had committed suicide.

The crown however, argued that Martyn killed Edith in a jealous rage, when he thought she might leave him for another man, and that he was guilty of wilful murder. His defence suggested that Edith was a quick tempered young woman, and that there had been a quarrel, but there was no intent to murder or otherwise harm her. It had been unintentional, and she had fallen to the ground dead, almost as soon as he touched her. The severe injuries it was claimed, had been caused after her death, as he desperately tried to divert suspicion by trying to make her death look like a suicide.

The jury retired but returned to the court on two occasions. The first was to seek clarification from the judge regarding the prisoner's intentions, and the second was to ask for the medical evidence to be repeated. They eventually returned with a guilty verdict and Martyn was sentenced to death.

Almost immediately, his solicitors, Messrs Banks, Kay and Redman organised a petition for a reprieve on the basis that he had been mentally ill and had been provoked into committing the crime. It read as follows:

Reg v Martyn

Signatories to the petition for a reprieve on the grounds that the jury's strong recommendation to mercy owing to the temperament of and provocation received by the said Walter Martyn and also on account of his youth.

Copies were sent to local mills and other work places, which led to more than 2,000 signatures being collected and forwarded to the Home Office. However, on the Saturday before the planned execution news was received that there would be no reprieve. His desperate supporters arranged a town meeting on the Sunday evening, 10 December 1911, at the United Methodist School on Bethel Street. This was attended by local MP Mr H T Cawley, who at the meeting's request presented another petition to the Home Secretary on the following day. This he did, but again it was refused and on Monday night, Martyn, who had been confident of a reprieve learnt that he would hang the following morning.

The hangman was to be John Ellis, but as he arrived at Strangeways Gaol on the eve of the execution, he had more than Martyn on his mind, for this was to be a double hanging. The next day he was to hang two men simultaneously, the first time this had occurred at Strangeways since 1884, and the second of only three such events at the gaol. Joining the Heywood murderer on the scaffold would be forty-one-year-old John Edward Tarkenter, condemned to death for the murder of his forty-two-year-old wife, Rosetta, at Heyside, near Oldham.

The Tarkenters married in June 1889, and for the first two years, they were apparently happy. However, after the birth of their son George, the relationship deteriorated, and he enlisted to escape the unhappy household. He served in the army for eleven years, and saw active service in South Africa during the Boer War. He then returned to Rosetta, and they decided that they would try and give their marriage another chance. He settled back into civilian life, and found work in his trade as a cotton spinner, but their relationship worsened, due mainly to his heavy drinking and violent temper.

They separated on four further occasions, the last time being in August 1910, when he entered the Stockport Workhouse. He returned to the family home at 2 Hilton Street, Royton, near Oldham in early July 1911, but this time the attempted reconciliation would end in tragedy. He continued to drink as heavily as ever, and he was unable to find work in any of the local cotton mills, which led to him having to resort to causal work at haymaking.

At 5 am on Tuesday 18 July, Tarkenter woke his son, George, who left for work after a few minutes. About one hour later, neighbour William Cuddy heard three screams, and told his wife 'That's Rosie screaming'. Afterwards, at about 8 am, William met Tarkenter leaving a local pub. Tarkenter said he was going to pawn several shawls to raise cash for alcohol. After he did so, the two men spent much of the day drinking together. Tarkenter told his companion that Rosetta was ill, and both of them returned to 2 Hilton Street. Tarkenter went upstairs, and returned to Cuddy a few minutes later to say that she was much better, although she was in fact dead by this time. The two men left the house and resumed their drinking for another few hours, before parting and making their way home. Tarkenter's decision to spend much of the day with his neighbour and to take him to his home, where Rosetta's body lay upstairs, was strange, given what was to emerge at the trial.

Tarkenter left his home at 3.45 pm and unexpectedly met his brother George on the street. He asked George for some money with which to buy more beer, but was refused as he was clearly already the worse for drink. Tarkenter responded by saying 'You may as well give it to me, for it is the last drink I shall have. I have murdered Rose.'

His brother did not believe him, and left him, but at 6.15 pm, Tarkenter's son returned home from work. There he found the front door locked, which was unusual. Having entered the house and finding nobody there, he became worried and went upstairs to his parents' bedroom. He was confronted by the sight of his mother lying on the bed which was saturated with blood, with her throat cut. He reported it immediately to the police, who arrested his father shortly afterwards.

Sergeant Taylor found Tarkenter drinking beer from a jug in the street. As the officer approached him Tarkenter said 'I know you have come for me. I know I have cut her bloody throat. I know I shall have to swing. I'll tell you what I did with the razor if you will pay me for a pint of beer.' The sergeant did not take him up on this offer, but as he detained him, his prisoner took a razor out of his pocket, saying 'I have done it with this.'

The police surgeon, Dr Kinnear, examined the body and found a seven inch gash across the victim's throat. It had been inflicted with such force that the jugular vein, larynx and gullet were completely severed. The body was cold and she had been dead for several hours. Also at the scene of the crime, the doctor found a bloodstained shirt, which was identified as belonging to Tarkenter.

The inquest was held on Thursday 20 July at Royston Police Court, with evidence being given by William Cuddy, Sergeant Taylor, and Tarkenter's brother. The prisoner's son George, in his testimony provided a possible motive for the crime, and the following exchange with the coroner took place:

Coroner: What was the cause of the trouble between your father and mother?

George: The last time he went away it was because she knew something about him, and she might tell me.

Coroner: Was he jealous of your mother?

George: Yes sir, very.

Coroner: Where any names mentioned?

George: Yes, he mentioned three.

Coroner: Was there any other cause?

George: Yes, he was very insulting and he raked old things up.

The coroner appears to have been satisfied that the prisoner was jealous and that this was the motive for the crime, but the 'something' the victim knew about her husband remained unknown; and why was Tarkenter worried that she might inform their son about it? A possible answer would be provided at his trial. The coroner's jury returned with a verdict of wilful murder, committed by Tarkenter, who was sent to the next Manchester Assizes on the coroner's warrant.

SON'S SHOCK.

Found His Mother Dead.

HEYSIDE TRAGEDY.

Wife Discovered With Throat Cut.

TO-DAY'S INQUEST EVIDENCE.

The coroner's jury committed Tarkenter for trial having found that she had been murdered by him.
The Manchester Evening Chronicle

Tarkenter appeared before the magistrates at the same venue on the following Saturday, when the police applied for a further remand to the local police cells for a few days while they completed their enquiries, and stated that no evidence would be offered at this hearing. When asked if he had any objections, the prisoner said he did. He had a large lump on his big toe, and complained that he was not receiving adequate medical treatment locally, and that he wished to be sent immediately to Strangeways. The police confirmed that they had made and applied a bread poultice the previous day, but it had not proved effective; however they undertook to provide medical assistance for him. As Tarkenter was complaining about his big toe, Rosetta was being buried at Shaw Church; and as for Strangeways? He would be there soon enough.

At the next magistrates' hearing on the following Tuesday, his son George gave similar evidence to that provided at the inquest. When he had completed it, the following interchange took place, which confirmed that it was not only Rosetta who was scared of this violent man:

Tarkenter: Have I ever molested you?

George: No, but you would have done if you had ever got the chance.

Chairman: What do you mean by that?

George: He would have assaulted me if I had not run out of his way. On one occasion I slept out all night through being frightened of him.

Tarkenter: That's enough; I've finished with him.

When Sergeant Taylor was giving his evidence about the prisoner's arrest, Tarkenter took exception to part of this evidence. He denied saying to the officer that he had cut her *bloody* throat. When the sergeant confirmed that he had in fact done so, the prisoner replied 'That's strange, because I always show respect for the dead.'

As the proceedings drew to a close, the chairman of the bench advised Tarkenter that a formal not guilty plea would be entered. The prisoner responded by complaining bitterly about a photograph of him in his army uniform which had been published in the press. He suggested that somebody had no doubt received payment for this, and he felt he should have the money to put towards his defence costs.

The chairman stated that it was nothing to do with this court, and he remanded Tarkenter in custody. A disgruntled prisoner had at least one wish fulfilled as he was now sent to Strangeways to await his trial, which took place on the day following that of Martyn at Manchester Assizes before the same judge. Gordon Hewart prosecuted and he was assisted by Mr Kennedy, and the defence was undertaken by Mr McLeary.

Although a formal not guilty plea had been entered, Takenter had never denied having killed Rosetta. This presented his barrister with some difficulties if he was to save his client's life. Mr McLeary's case was that there had been some provocation, which meant that the charge could be reduced to one of manslaughter. He therefore called Tarkenter to give evidence in his own defence, and he asked him to describe what happened on the day of Rosetta's killing.

The accused man told the court that he and Rosetta were on friendly terms that morning, and after George had gone to work, Rosetta asked him to fetch his cut throat razor so that she could cut her corns. When he returned to the bedroom with the razor, he claimed that her mood had swung violently. She began complaining and shouted at him 'I am sick of being without money; I am never without money while you are away.'

He described becoming angrier as what he described as her nagging continued, and she then made some comments that he acknowledged 'sent me off my head'. His barrister asked him for more details, but Tarkenter simply gave a large sigh and looked around the packed courtroom. The judge sensed what the problem was and asked the prisoner if he would prefer the court to be cleared of all of the women who were present, to which the prisoner said he would. And so it was that the large number of Edwardian ladies who were attending the trial, were ordered to leave the court, to ensure that they heard nothing that would offend them; no doubt they were extremely disappointed.

Tarkenter resumed his evidence from the dock by saying that Rosetta had threatened to leave him, and furthermore, she had been told by William Cuddy, that her husband 'Bothered with little children'. At this he lost his temper and all control of his actions, and he slashed her throat with the cut throat razor.

Having completed his evidence, the ladies were allowed back into the courtroom, in time to hear Mr McLeary's address to the jury. He claimed that his client had been severely provoked by Rosetta, and that meant that he should be convicted of the lesser offence of manslaughter. However, this argument was rejected by the judge in his summing up, and he advised the jury 'I must tell you, as a matter of law, that no such words as are alleged to have been used by the deceased woman to the prisoner, can be recognized as a provocation, which will reduce this offence. There is no suggestion of any violence, or any suggestion, except that of the prisoner, which he has made for the first time today'.

Ten minutes later, the jury returned with a guilty verdict, and as the judge was having the black cap placed on his head, the silence of the court was shattered by the scream of an unknown woman dressed in black, who then fainted. Eventually sentence of death was passed and the condemned man was taken back to Strangeways.

On the surface this appears to have been a straightforward case of a brutal and jealous husband murdering his wife with a cut throat razor, which was a commonly used weapon in domestic murders at the time. However, he was not drunk when he killed Rosetta, and jealousy might not have been the only motive he had. Was he a paedophile as William Cuddy is supposed to have told the

CONDEMNED MEN.

No Reprieve Efforts in Heyside Case.

Whilst active efforts are being made to secure a reprieve for Walter Martyn, of Heywood, who was sentenced to death at the Manchester Assizes for the murder of his sweetheart in Plumpton Wood, nothing has been done so far as is known in Manchester to start a similar movement on behalf of John Edward Tarkenter, the spinner, of Heyside, who was found guilty of murdering his wife on July 13. On inquiry at the office of Mr. McCleary, who defended Tarkenter at the Assizes, we were informed that there had been no application for an appeal, and further that nothing had been heard of a reprieve petition.

Determined efforts were made to save Martyn, but Tarkenter made it clear that he did not want a reprieve. Manchester Evening News dead woman, and did the killer fear exposure? And why did he take William Cuddy back to his house with Rosetta's body still in the bedroom? Did he in fact plan to murder William Cuddy also, but for some reason decided not to do so? We shall never know the answer to these questions, and there is no evidence that any such theory was followed up by the police.

As frantic efforts were being made by Martyn's supporters to save his life, no such efforts were being made on behalf of Tarkenter, who had made it clear to his family and to his solicitor, that he believed the sentence was a just one for what he had done, and he wished to die. He met with his brother and sisters, together with his son George on the eve of his execution. In a highly emotional meeting, he urged his son to avoid alcohol, and he expressed his gratitude to the prison officers who had been his companions whilst he had been in the condemned cell. He told his family that he would walk bravely to the scaffold.

Double executions were becoming rare events, and this may explain why for the first time ever, the High Sheriff of the County, Sir George Pilkington, attended in person, rather than following tradition by sending his deputy. In doing so, he caused something of a sensation, amongst the crowd of about 200, who had gathered at the main gate, by arriving at the gaol in a motor car.

The executions were completed without a hitch. The condemned men had been kept in separate cells throughout their detention. They met for the first time in the corridor as they walked to the execution shed. No words passed between them as they joined the silent procession, led by the prison

The efforts to gain a reprieve for Martyn were not successful. Manchester Evening News

HEYWOOD MURDERER.

Home Secretary Declines to Grant Reprieve.

The effort to secure a reprieve for Walter Martyn, of Heywood, who is under sentence of death for strangling his sweetheart, Edith Griffiths, in a wood at Heywood, has failed.

This morning Messrs. Banks, Kay, and Redman, Martyn's solicitors, have received a communication from the Home Office stating that the Secretary of State has given careful consideration to the petition submitted, but regrets that he has failed to discover any grounds for advising any interference with the due course of the law.

The execution will, therefore, take place at Strangeways gaol on Tuesday.

governor R D Cruikshank. As soon as the two men reached the scaffold hoods were placed over their heads and the ropes around their necks, and Ellis pulled the bolt.

The double execution was performed by John Ellis, who as this photograph shows, gave public demonstrations of his technique. Rochdale Local History Library

CHAPTER 7

Hyman Perdovitch and David Caplan The Russian Connection 1919

... Perdovitch and Caplan stood side by side on the scaffold, and both faced death bravely, at what proved to be the last double hanging at Strangeways.

Following a gap of eight years there was another double hanging, and by coincidence the two men, who were convicted of separate crimes, shared a Russian background.

It was a few minutes after 9 am on Friday 15 August that thirty-four-year-old Hyman Perdovitch rushed into Chapel Street Police Station, in Salford. He was in a highly agitated state, and told the duty officer, Constable Marsh, 'You want me don't you?' The officer asked 'What do I want you for?' Perdovitch explained that he had injured a man at his place of work, and he was therefore detained by the constable. Perdovitch pulled out what appeared to be a new penknife and handed it to Constable Marsh, who noticed there was blood on the blade.

Perdovitch explained that he had wounded his foreman, Solomon Franks in the waterproofing department of Wilkes Brothers, which was nearby. As Perdovitch was telling Constable Marsh this story, an ambulance had been called for, to take the assault victim to Salford Royal Hospital. However, nothing could be done for the very badly injured man who died

SALFORD WORKSHOP TRAGEDY.

FOREMAN DIES FROM WOUNDS.

A Surrender to the Police.

Inspector Mitchell and a staff of police officers are investigating the tragedy which occurred early this morning in one of the workshops of Messrs. Wilks Brothers, in Booth-street, a narrow thoroughfare, running from Chapel-street, near the Trinity Market.

Just before nine o'clock a man walked into the Chapel-street Police Station and, addressing P.C. Marsh said, "Do you want me?" Marsh replied, "What for?" and the man answered "That affair at Wilks's. If you don't want me now, you will do."

Perdovitch surrendered to the police minutes after committing the murder. Manchester Evening News

on arrival. He was found to have two wounds about the head and neck, which had apparently been caused by a knife.

A short time earlier, at 8.45 am, Solomon Franks was in the workshop of which he was in charge, at Wilkes Brothers factory. There were about forty men and women in his charge, and he often opened a door which led out into a yard to ventilate the workshop. To do so, he had to pass the bench at which Perdovitch was working, and on reaching the door, he bent down slightly to turn the handle. As he did so, Perdovitch left his bench and approached his foreman from behind. He appeared to whisper something in his ear, before what at first seemed to be punching him twice about the head with his clenched fist. However, when the foreman fell to the ground, blood could be seen flowing from the area of his head and neck, and it was realized by those who witnessed it that he had in fact been stabbed.

One of those who witnessed it was Nathan Lewis who worked at the bench next to the assailant. He said to Perdovitch 'Hyman, what have you done?' Perdovitch pointed down to his own leg and replied 'You know I am an injured man and you can see how he has been treating me. I have done it now, and am waiting for the police.'

Another workmate, Abraham Nelson, went over to the telephone to summon medical assistance and Perdovitch said to him 'I have finished him off. He deserved it.' By the time Abraham returned to the workshop, Perdovitch had left.

A few minutes later, Everard Newbold, who owned a tobacconists shop on Chapel Street, went to the front door, having seen the ambulance arrive at the factory. He found Perdovitch, whom he recognized as a customer, standing in the shop entrance. He asked him what had happened and received the reply 'Nothing worth talking about. The man is no good to anybody so I have done him in.' He then walked off in the direction of Chapel Street Police Station.

So what were the circumstances that had led to the brutal killing of his foreman, Solomon Franks? For the answers it is necessary to go back some time. Perdovitch had worked for Wilkes Brothers for several years before the outbreak of the Great War. In 1914 he tried to enlist, but he was turned down because he was Russian born, and despite the number of years spent in the United Kingdom, he was classed as a foreigner.

Although disappointed, the company received a large military order for waterproof garments, and he derived some satisfaction in being actively involved in something that was helping in the war effort. In 1915 he again attempted to enlist, but once again he was turned down. However, in 1916, at the third attempt, he was at last accepted by the 2nd Battalion, Royal Irish Regiment.

He served his adopted country well, until he was wounded in the left thigh at Ypres on 4 August 1917. He spent eleven days in a field hospital in France, before being sent to a military hospital in Bristol. He was subsequently discharged from the army on 15 August 1918.

On his return to Salford, he resumed work with his former employers, where he found himself under Solomon Franks who was to be his foreman. From the start the two men did not get on, and there was a good deal of friction between the pair.

The former soldier still needed treatment for his thigh wound, and arrangements were made for him to attend Salford Royal Hospital on a regular basis. The hospital was close by and he was to attend between 1.30 and 2 pm, so that he could receive the necessary treatment during his lunch break, and not lose any wages. It seems incredible nowadays that a former soldier suffering from a serious wound, received in battle, should be treated this way. However, that was how things were then and there was no complaint from Perdovitch. He took a meal with him to eat en route to the hospital, and he had his apprentice brew his tea at about ten minutes to one, so he could have a drink before setting off for his treatment. However, after a fortnight of this arrangement, his apprentice approached him and told him 'Mr Franks has given me a telling off, and would not let me brew the tea.'

Perdovitch took great exception at this, and asked his foreman to reconsider his decision, suggesting that their boss, Charlie Wilkes, would not object. The foreman's response however, was unsympathetic: 'Never mind Charlie, I am boss here.' Perdovitch remained calm, and said and did nothing to inflame the situation. He complained to his landlady, Mrs Reuben, who advised him to leave the company. If he had taken her advice, the events that followed might well have been avoided.

Several weeks passed without any further incidents, but Perdovitch felt further aggrieved when his foreman told him he had been a fool to volunteer to fight in the war. This was too much for the wounded former soldier, who told his foreman he would be making a complaint to their boss. He approached Charlie Wilkes and reported the foreman's comments. His boss was understanding, and promised to confront the other man.

After the foreman had been admonished by their boss Perdovitch became convinced that his foreman's attitude towards him worsened rather than improved. He felt that he was being given the worst paid work and the heaviest duties, regardless of his wound. Some colleagues, however, felt that

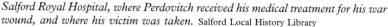

Salford Royal Hospital, where Perdovitch received his medical treatment for his war wound, and where his victim was taken. Salford Local History Library

these grievances were imagined, and that he was given duties similar to everyone else in the department. Martin Scheer, who had worked alongside Perdovitch for six weeks prior to the killing, did not believe him to have been unfairly treated. Another workmate, Nathan Lewis, also believed that the heavy work and least well paid tasks had been equally distributed amongst the men, and that their women colleagues had been allocated most of the relatively light work.

Imagined or not, his sense of grievance led Perdovitch to attack Solomon Franks in a particularly brutal fashion. The police were convinced that this was a premeditated act and that the intention had been to kill his victim. They had the several admissions of responsibility made by the accused man, but further confirmation was provided by the post-mortem findings and what he had said to one of his landlady's children on the day before the attack.

Dr Ghosh, resident surgeon at Salford Royal Hospital, confirmed that the victim was dead on arrival at the hospital, before any treatment could be given. He performed the post-mortem the following day. He found a wound just under two inches long, at the back of the neck, an inch below and one inch behind the lobe of the right ear. It was more than three inches deep, and divided all of the muscles at the back of neck. It had also penetrated between the first and second vertebrae, before damaging the spinal cord.

The second wound, a little over one inch in length, was located in the middle of the back of the neck, and was more than two inches deep. The cause of death was shock and haemorrhage arising from the wounds, which had been caused by a sharp instrument, like the penknife found on the accused man at the time of his arrest. The nature of the wounds and their depth indicated to Dr Ghosh that they had been inflicted with great force.

The fact that the accused man's sense of grievance towards the deceased had been building up for some time, did not in itself prove premeditation. However, the police produced a witness whom they believed proved that Perdovitch knew on the previous day that he intended killing his supposed tormentor. This was Rebecca Reuben, the teenage daughter of

FOREMAN KILLED.

SALFORD WORKSHOP TRAGEDY.

Prisoner Remanded.

At Salford, to-day Hyman Perdovitch, of Albert Avenue, Sedgley Park, was charged with unlawfully causing the death of Solomon Franks, of Bellott-street, Cheetham, by stabbing him in the neck with a knife at the waterproof manufactory of Messrs. Wilks Bros., in Booth-street, S... i, yesterday.

The justices were Mr. C. C. Goodwin, Mr. A. Willett, and Mr. G. Perry.

Superintendent Clark stated that the prisoner left the firm mentioned to join the forces, and was injured at the front, for which he was in receipt of a pension. He received his discharge and was taken back again by Messrs Wilks Brothers. The dead man was the foreman of the department where the prisoner was employed as a machinist.

Shortly before 9 o'clock yesterday morning Mr. Franks went to open one of the windows because of the heat. The prisoner was seen to leave his machine, and the workpeople thought he was leaning over and talking to Mr. Franks.

The prisoner made two blows at the man's neck, but the startled onlookers saw no weapon used. Mr. Franks, however, collapsed, and it was then found that he was bleeding from wounds in the neck. The ambulance was sent for and the man conveyed to the Salford Royal Hospital, where he expired directly after arrival

Perdovitch was committed to face trial at the Manchester Assizes. Manchester Evening News

his landlady. She returned home on the day before the killing and Perdovitch gave her half a crown, telling her that he was going on his holidays the following day. When she asked where he was going, he replied 'Strangeways'. This was enough to convince the police that he was guilty of premeditated murder, and this view was agreed with by the coroner's jury at the inquest.

His trial took place on 5 December 1919 at the Manchester Assizes, before Mr Justice McCardie. He was represented by Mr Lustgarten and the prosecution was conducted by Mr Saul and Mr Jordan.

From the time he walked into the police station on Chapel Street, just minutes after the attack, the prisoner had never denied responsibility for the crime. Even at the committal hearing before the Salford Magistrates' Court he had declared 'All I can say is I have been driven to it'.

At the trial, his defence was that it had been an accident. It was claimed that he had bought the penknife to use at work, and he was holding it in his hand at the time of the killing. His foreman had noticed it in his hand, and had seemingly become worried and lunged at the accused. Perdovitch had moved to the side, and the deceased had stumbled and fallen onto the knife.

This fanciful explanation was rejected by the jury, who found him guilty, but with a strong recommendation for mercy.

Great efforts were made to secure a reprieve for Perdovitch, despite his having murdered a family man with five children for what many believed were imaginary grievances. Nevertheless, the war was still fresh in the minds of people and the first anniversary for the Armistice had recently passed. There was widespread sympathy for this foreigner, who had volunteered to serve the country, despite early setbacks when he first attempted to do so. Furthermore, he had been wounded in battle.

The petition was organized by Mrs Wright, landlady of the *Punch Bowl Hotel*, where the condemned man had been a regular customer. Twenty-two thousand signatures were collected, and there was a feeling of optimism about the chances of a reprieve. Mrs Wright was a regular visitor to Strangeways as was his former employer Charlie Wilkes and his wife, together with Rabbi Jacob Phillips of the Park Place Synagogue.

The petition to save Perdovitch was organised by Mrs Wright, landlady of the Punch Bowl Hotel. Salford Local History Library

Perdovitch spent his time writing letters and poetry, one of which reflected his strong feelings of pride he had for the United Kingdom, and which was entitled 'Armistice Day':

On the fateful morning, the eleventh of November,
When British might was proof
Coming generations will always remember
When the Hun called 'Halt I've had enough

In Europe's trial, in her darkest hour
In civilisation's greatest distress
She fought and held the Brute's power
Answered small nations SOS

On the eleventh of November, at the eleventh hour
A silent thought of those Divine
For those that fought the Brute power
Until the Union Jack kept watch on the Rhine

However, the petition failed and Perdovitch was informed that he would hang on Tuesday 6 January 1920. John Ellis was to be in charge of the execution, but as this was to be double hanging he had the help of two assistants rather than one. They were Robert Baxter of Brighton and Edward Taylor, who travelled from St Albans. The man who would stand on the scaffold with Perdovitch however, had little public sympathy, and no significant attempt was made to save him.

His name was David Caplan, who nine years earlier, when he was aged thirty-three had married Freda Waterman. For the first two years they lived in the home of Miriam, Freda's mother in Liverpool. Eventually the couple moved to Leeds, where he found work as a machinist.

They had two children, Herman and Maurice, but because of his frequent violent outbursts, Freda returned to her mother's home on no fewer than seven occasions. However, on each occasion she was persuaded by her husband to return, if not for his sake, then for the sake of the children.

In June 1919 the Caplans returned to Liverpool, and after a brief stay with Freda's mother, they moved into 141 West Derby Road, where Freda opened a millinery shop. His violence continued however, and in August 1919, he again assaulted her. This time she had had enough, and she threatened him with the police, which she had not done in the past. At this he screamed at her 'If you go to the police I will kill you and harm the shop.'

Freda did not contact the police on this occasion, and her sister Minnie was invited to stay with them, ostensibly to help with the children whilst Freda looked after the shop. It was also probably to try and prevent her husband assaulting her again. If this was the intention, it failed. On 9 September, after asking him for money, he responded by assaulting her yet again.

Freda now made an official complaint to the police, and Caplan appeared at the local magistrates' court where he was fined ten shillings for the assault. Even at court he threatened revenge and shouted 'I'll swing for it'.

She was subsequently granted a separation order, and custody of both children, Herman who was now a six-year-old, and three-year-old Maurice. This followed another particularly violent assault during which Caplan hit his wife with a brush and threatened to cut Minnie's throat if she was a witness against him.

The terms of the order were that he could have access to the children, and he would receive £20 from Freda. He was required to leave 141 West Derby Road by 20 October 1919.

Tragically, rather than solve her problems, the separation order served to increase his sense of resentment towards his wife, and in fuelling a need for revenge. This he would have in a terrible and horrific manner.

On the evening of Monday 13 October, Caplan met a group of friends for a drink in a local pub. To his friends he appeared calm and he had not drunk to excess when he said he was going home. A few hours later, at 6 am, neighbours heard screams and groans from the Caplan house, but assumed it was just another of their arguments.

Later that day, Freda's brother Myer called at the house, and was concerned not to receive any reply. He went to the back of the house and found an open window, which led into the scullery, and through which he gained entry.

In the house, he first of all found his brother-in-law, downstairs, with his throat cut but still alive. A horrified Myer went upstairs and found Freda and the children with severe head injuries. The children were dead but Freda was still breathing, albeit with great difficulty. As he left the house to summon help, a distraught Myer glared at Caplan, saying 'You have done this.' There was no reply and Caplan simply turned his head to one side, avoiding the other man's eyes.

Freda died the following day, and post-mortems were performed on the three victims by Dr W G Roberts. He found that each victim had been severely beaten about the head. He also discovered that the beating had been of such ferocity that the skulls of the two children had been rammed several inches into their brains.

The police found the murder weapon used in all three crimes in the house, which was a bloody iron. It did not take the police much time to confirm Myer's view that Caplan had killed all three of his family, before cutting his own throat.

It is probable that this was a genuine suicide bid by the killer, as he did not suffer superficial wounds. He had to spend two weeks in hospital, during which time he had a permanent police guard by his bed. For the first week he remained silent but he later began discussing the killings with the police officers at his bedside. He insisted he could remember nothing about the killings but accepted responsibility for them. He told one officer that if he had indeed killed the children he deserved to die.

He was arrested on his discharge from hospital and charged with the three murders. Following the inquests on the victims and his appearance before the local magistrates, he was committed to the Manchester Assizes, where his trial took place on 2 December 1919, before Mr Justice McCardie. Mr Merriman and Douglas Stuart represented the Crown, and Mr Madden defended.

The compelling case of the prosecution was put to the jury, and the defence relied on an insanity plea. One of their witnesses was Harris Zermanski of Leeds, who was married to one of the accused's cousins. He had himself been assaulted by Caplan in the past, and had also been threatened by him with a knife. He therefore had first-hand knowledge of his violence, and he also had information about the prisoner's family background in Russia. He told the court that Caplan's mother had been committed to a lunatic asylum. His brother Moses had been called up into the Russian army, only to be discharged soon afterwards for what the witness described as 'acting madly'. He also confirmed that when the prisoner was employed as a machinist in Leeds, his nickname had been 'Mad Dave'.

However, the jury was not convinced and Caplan was found guilty and sentenced to death.

The county sheriff and the judges arrive at the opening of the 1919 Winter Assizes. Manchester Evening News

At 8 am on Tuesday 6 January 1920 Perdovitch and Caplan stood side by side on the scaffold, and both faced death bravely, at what proved to be the last double hanging at Strangeways.

CHAPTER 8

John Horner
The Salford Sex Murderer
1924

A most cruel and most wanton crime.

It was 2.15 pm on Tuesday 10 June 1924, as Harold Pinchin arrived home to be greeted by his son, Norman. The little boy, who had celebrated his fifth birthday two weeks earlier, rushed up to his father and asked him for a penny. Harold had only a halfpenny, which he gave to his son, who rushed off in the direction of a nearby sweet shop with his pal, eight-year-old Eric Wilson. Harold heard his son shouting 'Come along Eric, we've got a halfpenny'.

It was to be the last time he would hear his son's voice, and see him alive, for later that day Harold was contacted at his workplace to be informed that the lad was dead, and he was required at the mortuary to identify the body. Later, as he looked down at his son's young face, it was realized that Norman had died in suspicious circumstances, but the true horror of those circumstances, were at that stage still unknown.

After he had left his father, Norman and Eric had made their way to Peel Park, where they decided to play in the summer shed. They had not been there very long, when a man they did not know approached them. He asked the boys if they wanted to go to the canal which was close by, to look at the water, and as he did so he grabbed Norman's hand.

Eric, being that little bit older than Norman, seemed instinctively to know that something was seriously wrong. As he moved away, the stranger tried to reassure him. He gave the older boy fourpence and told him to go and buy two ice creams. Eric asked Norman to come with him, but the man would not

Peel Park was the scene of a crime that shocked the nation. Salford Local History Library

release his grip of the younger boy's hand. Eric went for the ice creams, but when he returned to the spot where he had left the other two, there was no sign of them. He looked for a few minutes, but it started to rain so he made his way home.

The man had taken Norman to the canal towpath at Windsor Bridge and, as they walked there, they were seen by fourteen-year-old Norman Thomas, who knew the boy but not the man with him.

They were also seen by Harry Barnes, who worked at Ashton's sawmill on Wallness Road, near to the bridge. That afternoon he was sat on the timber yard wall, waiting for the newspaper boy. From his position he had a clear view of the pair walking towards the bridge. He lost sight of them as they walked under it, but thought nothing of it. However, ten minutes later he was astonished to see the man emerge from under the bridge; he was carrying the boy, and threw him into the canal. The man knelt down, peering into the water, and after a few moments he stood up and began walking away from the spot.

A stunned Harry Barnes ran towards the bridge and, as he did so, the man walked past him quite calmly, but no words were spoken between the two men. When he arrived at the bridge Harry looked for the boy but could see no sign of him. He decided to seek help and retraced his steps so that he was following the man.

He followed him along Wallness Road and on to The Crescent. He was walking towards Manchester, but Harry saw two policemen and called out to them. He told Constables Walter Smith and James Lorison his strange tale, and the three of them caught up with the man. Harry said 'I saw this man throw a little boy in the canal', to which the man replied 'I have done nothing of the kind', and he attempted to punch his accuser.

The four of them went to the spot where the incident was said to have happened, but nothing could be found. Nevertheless, the man was detained and taken to Salford Town Hall to await questioning whilst further enquiries were made, and the canal was dragged.

The man being held by the police was twenty-three-year-old John Charles Horner, a single man, who lived with his parents in Lissadel Street, Pendleton. He had been raised in a hard working and respectable family, and received loving support from his parents. On one occasion, when he was out of work, his parents had bought him a horse and cart; when the horse was found to be ill, they bought him another one. When he was unemployed, they kept him.

Gradually, details of the crime emerged.
Manchester Evening News

TRAGIC PASSING OF A SALFORD BOY.

Appalling Allegation Against Pendleton Man.

THROWN INTO CANAL!
—*Police Charge.*

Dog Which Mourned Loss of His Curly-headed Playmate.

THERE is a wealth of pathos in the tragic passing of little Norman Pinchin, the curly-headed five-year-old Salford boy, whose drowning in the London, Midland and Scottish Railway Co.'s canal at Salford there was an echo at the local police court, to-day.

The whole district in which "Copper," as the little chap was called was known, shares his parents' grief, and a pathetic figure at the home to-day was "Billy," a champion Airedale, with whom the boy had attended many dog shows, who seemed to miss his little playmate.

Not a whit less sensational than the startling recovery from the canal of the lifeless body of the boy was the dramatic appearance at the Salford Police Court to-day of a young man charged with causing the death of the boy.

The court was appalled by the story unfolded by Police Inspector Smith and by the repetition of a statement alleged to have been made by an eye-witness—"the prisoner . . . . deliberately threw him (the boy) into the canal."

HANDSOME PRISONER.
Police Officer's Story of Meeting in Peel Park.

However, he was known to the police, and although there was no record of any violence, he had been convicted of theft. As recently as December 1923 he had been sentenced to six months' imprisonment for stealing jewellery and other valuables from his parents.

As Horner was being taken into custody, Constable Smith had rushed to the Crescent Police Station for some grappling irons, with which he dragged the canal near to Windsor Bridge. After about thirty minutes, he found Norman's body. The officer made desperate efforts at artificial respiration at the scene and in the ambulance as it sped towards Salford Royal Hospital. Unfortunately, these efforts were unsuccessful, and he was taken to the mortuary to await identification and a post-mortem.

However, the police did not wait for the results of the post-mortem, and arranged an identification parade which was held at the town hall at 8.25 pm on the night of Norman's death. It was arranged by Detective Inspector Jowett, who enlisted the help of nine men to stand in the line-up. However, Horner objected to one of them, and he was removed. The inspector asked if he was satisfied, but Horner insisted on being allowed to wash. This was agreed to and on his return he placed himself near to the end of the line of men. Horner was picked out by all of the witnesses.

When Norman's body was pulled from the canal, he was found to be wearing a blue jersey, and white woollen underpants, which were unfastened thus exposing the area around his genitals. Beneath his jersey, his braces were still in place, but were no longer fastened to his trousers, which were missing. These were found at 3 am the next morning during a second search of the canal, and it was clear he had not been wearing them at the time he had been thrown into the canal.

The true motive for the crime was beginning to emerge, and the worst fears of the investigating police officers were confirmed at the post-mortem.

This was performed by Dr Stanley Hodgson on the day following the crime. He found that Norman had been a healthy, well developed and well nourished little boy. He confirmed that the boy had not drowned as first thought, as there was no water in his lungs. The examination revealed that Norman had been brutally sodomized, which had resulted in his suffering severe shock, which had killed him.

The inquest was held on the following Friday before the coroner Mr Holmes, and rumours about what had happened to the dead little boy had been spreading throughout the district. Many hundreds of people gathered at the town hall, but not all could gain admission. This led to a large and angry crowd outside of the building. Inside, the victim's parents were being supported by friends and relatives, but they were still visibly distressed, and finding it to be an ordeal.

His father, Harold, was called to provide evidence of identification, but on seeing the accused in the dock, he had to be restrained as he shouted 'You swine. If I could get my hands on you.' Horner remained apparently unmoved, as he would do at all of the public hearings he was present at.

The coroner's jury viewed the body, and heard the evidence of those who had witnessed the events surrounding the boy's death, together with the testimony of Dr Hodgson regarding the post-mortem. The jury retired for four minutes before returning with a verdict of wilful murder.

By the time the proceedings had concluded, a crowd estimated at 3,000 people was assembled outside of the building. As the accused emerged from it, protected by several police officers, the crowd pressed forward shouting abuse at Horner, amid cries of 'Let's get him' and 'Drown him'.

When the formal hearing to commit Horner to the Assizes for trial was held a few days later, much of the same evidence as that presented at the inquest was heard. However, there was a significant event involving the boy Eric Wilson. He was asked by the magistrate if he could identify the man who had approached Norman and him in the park on 10 June. There was no immediate response, and it was discovered that Eric was short sighted. He was invited to walk around the court room and, as he approached the dock, he pointed to Horner and shouted 'That's him'.

Norman's funeral took place on Saturday 21 June, and thousands of people lined the route to Peel Green Cemetery, reflecting the shock felt at the nature of the offence and the sympathy felt for the victim's family. The cortège first of all made its way from the family home to Christ Church where the service was led by Reverend R W Thornhill, who could hardly be heard above the sound of sobbing.

There were many wreaths and some of the messages read 'In loving memory of little Ginger', and 'To a dear little pal from his playmates'. Others were sent from the scholars of Christ Church Sunday School, Hulme Street Infants, and Salford Fire Brigade. There was a special one from his friend which read 'To my

CANAL TRAGEDY.

Crowd's Last Tribute to Boy Victim.

IMPRESSIVE FUNERAL.

Streets Lined with Sorrowing Public.

Rarely can there have been a deeper or more sincere manifestation of public sympathy than was shown to-day at the funeral of Norman Pinchin, the five-years-old boy, of Crescent View, Salford, whose body was recovered from the local canal under such tragic circumstances.

It seemed as though the whole district was in mourning for "Copper," as the sunny-haired little fellow was known.

Thousands of people lined the route of the funeral cortège. Manchester Evening News

dear little playmate, from Eric and his father'. A particularly large and attractive wreath was meant specifically for Mrs Pinchin, and it read 'To a mother, from the mothers of Park Place'.

Horner's trial took place on 17 July at the Manchester Assizes, with Mr Justice Talbot presiding. The prosecution was led by William Madden KC, who was assisted by Hugh Beatley; the defence barrister was Mr McKeever.

In his opening address to the jury, Mr Madden outlined the prosecution case which, he emphasized, was supported by eyewitnesses; this was that Norman had been subjected to a horrible outrage, by the prisoner in the dock, who when he realized the boy was dead, threw him into the canal. Horner was, he stated, responsible for 'A most cruel and most wanton crime'. The crown's witnesses were those heard at the preliminary hearings, and nothing new was added to the case.

The defence case rested solely on the claim that their client was the victim of mistaken identity. Mr McKeever highlighted some discrepancies in the evidence provided by the eight and fourteen-year-old witnesses. Furthermore he urged the jury members to ask themselves if credence could be given to the evidence of a short sighted eight-year-old. He also reminded them that Norman Thomas had only had a fleeting glimpse of the man who was with the victim, and he could not therefore be certain it had been Horner.

Harry Barnes, however, was no child, and he had had a relatively lengthy period of time to see the man who had been with Norman on the canal towpath. The barrister attempted to discredit his evidence and there was a heated exchange between the two men. This was when Mr McKeever implied that the witness must have known at the time that Horner was not that man. It was accepted by all concerned that the killer had walked towards the witness from the direction of the crime, and had indeed passed Mr Barnes. However, this did not in itself mean that his client was the man. The barrister continued by saying that the witness agreed that the killer walked past with an unconcerned and relaxed air about him; furthermore, he continued, would not Harry Barnes have confronted him if he had indeed felt he had been responsible for throwing a child into the canal. Harry Barnes retorted that he had had to use his own judgement at the time, and his main concern was to try and save the child, hence his decision to rush to the scene.

Horner was later called to the stand to give evidence on his own behalf. He remained composed, as usual, and he was called mainly to give an explanation of his movements during the afternoon in question, and why he was by the side of the canal in that specific area at that particular time.

He told the court that he and his girlfriend, Sarah Verity, had been courting for seven years. She worked as a wardmaid at Salford Royal Hospital and, on 10 June, they had arranged to meet as it was her day off. They planned to meet at Old Trafford railway station at 3 pm. He arrived at 2.55 pm, and waited for just ten minutes. It was raining, and he realized she would not come, so he took a tram and headed for the hospital. He got off the tram at the top of Oldfield Road, opposite the hospital, and by then it was 3.25 pm. He knew she would be taking her tea at 4 pm, and decided to take a walk as he waited for her to go to the dining room as he was not allowed to go to her room, in the hospital.

He approached the canal towpath from the direction of Oldfield Road, and thus walked to Windsor Bridge from the opposite direction to that stated by the witnesses. As he walked along the towpath he noticed nothing suspicious. The only person he saw was Harry Barnes, who ran past him, in the direction of the bridge, without saying a word. When he was approached later by the police officers, he was walking along The Crescent in the direction of the hospital, to meet Sarah.

Miss Verity was called as a witness and verified what Horner had said about their plans to meet that afternoon. She confirmed that she had not turned up because of the rain, and also that she was expecting him to come to the hospital at 4 pm, when she was due to have her tea.

In his summing up, the judge focused on the fact that it was accepted by both the prosecution and defence that the victim had died as a result of shock following a sexual assault. Therefore, murder was the correct charge that whoever was responsible should face, and this was even if it had not been the intention of the attacker to kill the victim.

The main question facing the jury was to decide whether or not it was the prisoner in the dock who had been responsible. In the absence of forensic evidence, the prosecution case was based largely on eyewitness accounts, and the defence case was that their client was innocent and was facing trial because of mistaken identity. The jury took sixty-five minutes to reach their verdict of guilty.

Horner appealed against his conviction, and it was heard in London at the Court of Criminal Appeal, on Monday 28 July. The Lord Chief Justice, Lord Hewart, presided, and the other judges were Mr Justice Shearman and Mr Justice Sankey; the same prosecution and defence barristers from the trial represented the crown and Horner.

The appeal judges stated that the whole case rested on the identification of Horner as the man who was with the victim. As far as they were concerned, there was sufficient reliable eyewitness evidence, and the court had no doubt regarding the prisoner's guilt, and the appeal was dismissed.

It is hardly surprising that given the nature of the crime he was convicted of, there was no public support for a reprieve. However, the condemned man's father wrote a personal plea to the Home Secretary but this was unsuccessful.

In his final days in the condemned cell he remained stoical, but his father reported that he broke down just once. His son wept and burying his head in his hands cried 'I would not have cared what they did at me had I done it, but I didn't do it.'

Although there was little sympathy for Horner, there was to be a final act of compassion. His mother made her last visit to see him on the Monday before the execution. This was against the advice of her doctor, but she was determined to see him. The visit took place in a large visiting room, with mother and son sitting at opposite ends of a long table so that they were unable to touch each other in any way. At the end of the visit, the prison chaplain asked her if she would like to kiss her son for the last time. Breaking with tradition and also in contravention of prison rules, they were allowed to embrace.

On Wednesday 13 August 1924 Horner walked firmly to the gallows, still protesting his innocence of this ghastly crime.

CHAPTER 9

Buck Ruxton
The Horror in Dalton Square
1936

Six thousand people signed the petition for a reprieve, many of them from Lancaster, who could not believe he could have committed such terrible crimes.

The execution of Dr Buck Ruxton, one bright spring morning in 1936 brought to an end what was one of the most sensational murder cases of the decade.

He was born Bukhtyar Rustomji Ratanji Hakim on 27 March 1899, in Bombay. His father was a doctor, and he was raised in comfortable surroundings. He was an excellent student, and he was sent to London, arriving on Armistice Day in 1918, to complete his studies, graduating in 1922 with a Bachelor of Medicine and a Bachelor of Surgery, having also gained distinctions in midwifery and medical jurisprudence.

He joined the Indian Medical Service, and served in Basra and Baghdad. He left in 1925, and on his return to Bombay, with the rank of Captain, he married Motiabai J Ghadiali, the daugher of a wealthy clockmaker. However, the doctor was keen to improve his qualifications and he returned to the United Kingdom to study for a higher degree. However, he failed to qualify as a surgeon to enable him to practice in the United Kingdom, at both Edinburgh and London.

Whilst studying in Edinburgh he often visited a cafe on Leith Street, where he met Isabelle Van Ess, who was working as a waitress. When she was an eighteen-year-old she had married

Dr Buck Ruxton. Author's collection

a Dutch sailor but the relationship failed, and her husband had returned to Holland. Ruxton and Isabelle became lovers, but from the start he would become extremely jealous if she so much as spoke to another man, or even if he noticed her smiling at a male customer.

Nevertheless, the relationship flourished and in 1927 they moved to London, where he found work in practices in Walthamstow and Stepney. It was at this time that Isabelle travelled to Holland to obtain a divorce.

Ruxton, who at this stage was still known by his original name, was a vain man, who had expensive tastes. This was especially so as far as clothes were concerned, and he accumulated massive debts. He wrote to his wife in India, asking her and her family to send him £500. This request was refused and just £80 was sent to him. It was this rebuff that prompted him to break all contacts with his relatives in India and with the Indian community in London. He changed his name by deed poll to Buck Ruxton.

Isabelle was unaware of his first marriage, when she and Ruxton married by declaration under Scottish law. She gave birth to their first child in August 1929, and he seems to have realized that it was time to settle down, and that he needed a practice of his own. And so it was that in August 1930, this exotic couple and their child arrived at his newly purchased rooms at 2 Dalton Square, Lancaster.

They quickly settled into their new lives, and the dapper Ruxton became immensely popular in the town and the numbers on his patient list grew. He was known affectionately as 'The Rajah' and he prospered so much with Isabelle's help that he was soon earning as much as £3,500 annually. They had two more children but their relationship was nevertheless a volatile one, arising from his feelings of intense jealousy, due to his worries about her having relationships with other men. He also believed that she had attempted to poison him on one occasion, but it was his regular use of violence against her that led her to leave him on several occasions. However, she was persuaded each time to return to him and the children.

The police were called to the house on several occasions due to their loud and violent arguments. Such an occasion was on 6 April 1934, when he had again accused her of being unfaithful. It was as the police were leaving, having calmed the situation, that he said in the presence of the officers 'I would be justified in murdering her'.

Isabelle often sought shelter with her sister Jeannie Nelson, who lived in Edinburgh, and theirs was a close relationship. They decided to spend a few days in Blackpool together, and they booked into a boarding house for two nights. They spent Saturday 14 September 1935 enjoying the resort's many attractions; Jeannie returned to the boarding house, but Isabelle decided to drive the short journey to Lancaster. They arranged to meet in Blackpool the following day, but Isabelle did not turn up. Jeannie assumed that there had been another argument, and that her sister had probably decided to stay at home to reduce the tension.

The reason that Isabelle had not returned to Blackpool on the following day was because during the night of September 14 and 15, she had been murdered by her husband. During the next few days he dismembered her body and his other victim, Mary Rogerson, their housemaid, and drove them to the Scottish border area where he disposed of the body parts. He also set about finding explanations for the two women being missing.

The first person he had to convince was the cleaner, Mrs Oxley, who was due to arrive at the Ruxton home at 8 am on the Sunday morning. The doctor visited the charwoman's home at 6.30 am, to say that his wife and Mary had travelled to Edinburgh and that there was no need to clean the house.

However, the reason he did not want her at the house was because the bodies were still there and there was a large amount of blood he had yet to clean up.

At 10 am he told Miss Hanson, who delivered milk to the house, that the two women had taken the three children to Edinburgh with them. This was the first of his many mistakes in attempting to divert suspicion from himself. Police later established that the children were still in the house, but had been prevented from seeing the scene of the murders, of which they were unaware; they were left later that day with a friend, dentist Herbert Anderson.

That evening, he called at the home of Mary Rogerson's parents in Morecambe, to inform them that she had decided to accompany Isabelle to Edinburgh for a holiday and she would not be home for several days. At this stage, the Rogersons were not suspicious and took the doctor at his word. However, as the days passed without any word from their daughter, which was unusual, their concerns grew. The Rogersons were to visit Ruxton a few days later, and he changed his story to say that she had been having a secret romance with a laundry boy; she found that she was pregnant, and he and Isabelle had offered to help her arrange an abortion. Not wishing to involve Ruxton, they had arranged for it to be done in Edinburgh and this was the reason, he suggested, that she had not contacted them. However, they were not satisfied with this explanation, and reported her as a missing person on 9 October.

Ruxton had also written to Jeannie Nelson, his sister-in-law in Edinburgh. He wrote that Isabelle was hoping to become the Lancashire agent for a Scottish football pools entrepreneur, William Murphy, and she had travelled to Edinburgh to meet him. He also told her that he believed that she was on the point of leaving him, and was planning to travel to Canada to stay with relatives. Furthermore, he repeated the story about Mary being pregnant and Isabelle offering to help her arrange an abortion.

Jeannie was not persuaded by Ruxton's claims, especially as her sister had told her that she was indeed planning to leave him, but this would only be after she had raised sufficient funds to open a boarding house in Edinburgh.

Meanwhile, the whole country was both appalled and fascinated by the news of the dismembered bodies being discovered on the Scottish border. They had been found on Sunday 29 September at a place known as the *Devil's Beef Tub*, two miles from Moffatt. Susan Johnson and her mother were enjoying a morning walk, and as they crossed Gardenholme Bridge, Susan saw what she thought was a human arm below. Looking more carefully she saw what appeared to be other body parts spread over a wide area. The police were called, and the incredulous local officers discovered a large quantity of dismembered and mutilated human remains; there were so many, that it was not known initially how many bodies had been cut up.

Two upper arms and four pieces of flesh were found wrapped in a yellow blouse; two thigh bones, two legs and nine pieces of flesh had been placed in a pillow slip; also, seventeen pieces of flesh were wrapped in a cotton sheet. A torso and two legs, tied together by a piece of hem from a cotton sheet were found, as were two heads, one of which was wrapped in a pair of child's rompers. In some of the bundles, scraps of newspaper were discovered, and these proved invaluable in pointing to the person responsible.

Body parts continued to be found over the following days, and not just by the police. Farmers and ramblers found many more, and as late as 28 October a roadman found a left foot, nine miles distant, and on 4 November a woman found a right forearm and hand.

All of the remains were taken to the University of Edinburgh, where a team of leading medical experts was assembled, under the leadership of John Glaister, Professor of Forensic Medicine at Glasgow University, and James Couper Bash, Professor of Anatomy at Edinburgh.

The bodies were found to be well developed and well nourished, but they remained unidentified, and were known as Body Number 1 and Body Number 2. Each was allocated a box, into which, what were thought to be their respective parts were placed. Both heads had been mutilated by the removal of ears, eyes, noses, lips, and facial skin. Several teeth had been extracted, apparently after death. The less mutilated head was that of number 1, and at first the head of Body Number 2 was thought to be that of a man. Other parts had been removed, including the finger tips and ends of the toes of Number 2. A picture began to emerge of a deliberate attempt to prevent identification by finger prints or distinguishing marks. Other parts appear to have been removed and otherwise disposed of to prevent discovery of the cause of death, although there were indications that Number 1 had suffered two blows to the head.

Despite these attempts to mislead and confuse the investigators, and despite the limitations of forensic science even as late as the mid-1930s, valuable information was obtained. For instance, on Body 1 the upper arm bore four distinctive vaccination marks, and it also proved possible to take some incomplete finger and palm prints, which although would be insufficient for use in court, would help in identifying the person.

The medical team was eventually able to describe Body Number 1 as being that of a young woman aged about twenty-five, and about five feet tall. Body Number 2 was that of a more mature woman aged between thirty-five and forty years, and also five feet tall. All of the nation's police forces were sent these descriptions, and it immediately raised the suspicions of Lancaster's Chief Constable Vann, who had by then become aware of the two missing women from 2 Dalton Square.

A firm conclusion of the Edinburgh team was that the dismemberment and deliberate mutilation of the two bodies had been carried out by someone with a great deal of medical and anatomical knowledge. They were found to have been dismembered by the use of a saw, but were cut neatly into small parts, so as to be carried more easily. Furthermore, the absence of significant amounts of blood at the scene of their discovery, suggested that the bodies had been drained of blood, probably at the scene of their deaths. This would have been a particularly messy process for anyone unaware of how to perform the task, which would have taken two or three days.

Ruxton became aware that rumours were circulating the town that the bodies found in Scotland, were those of Isabelle and Mary, but he was unaware that the police suspected him right up until the time of his arrest. The investigations by the

Lancaster police were initially very discreet. However they had found evidence of unusual and suspicious behaviour in the days that followed the disappearances, and later they would find incriminating evidence at 2 Dalton Square, together with evidence linking him to the bodies.

The wrappings used for the parcels of body parts provided much useful information. Mary's mother identified the blouse as one she had bought in 1934 at a Morecambe jumble sale, and she recognised it by the patch she had sewn under the left armpit; she had given it to Mary, who had taken it with her to 2 Dalton Square. The rompers were shown to have been given to Mary by a Mrs Holmes of Grange-over-Sands, who was able to identify them as she had removed the original elastic and replaced it with distinctive string which was still in place. Mrs Oxley told the police that she had seen them in Mary's room at Dalton Square.

Four of the pieces of cotton sheet and a piece of hem found with the body parts, were sent to F W Barwick, Director of the Trinity House Laboratory, Manchester. He was also sent a complete cotton sheet from the Ruxton household and was asked to compare them. He compared the weave, weight, threads per inch, and turns per inch amongst other factors, and although he advised the police that he could not positively state they were from the same source, he described finding many similarities between the two sets of material.

Some accounts of the Ruxton case highlight the significance of the use of maggots found in the decomposing flesh of the body parts, in determining the length of time that they had been at the location where they were discovered. However their role was not pivotal, although they did confirm the time span, which was provided from other sources. The maggots, which were identified as those of the common bluebottle, were examined by Dr Alexander Mears of the Institute of Hygiene at Glasgow University, who found that they had been laid in the flesh about twelve to fourteen days before they were discovered. This was corroboration for the police theory that the parts had been dumped during the early hours of 16 September, and over the following few days.

The presence of bluebottle maggots helped to confirm when the body parts had been dumped. Richard Seed

Probably the most crucial evidence in determining the length of time they had been there were the scraps of newspaper found with them. They also provided compelling evidence of their origins. Scraps of the *Daily Herald* and *Sunday Chronicle* were found, dating from August to September 1935, together with pages from the *Sunday Graphic* and *Sunday News* dated Sunday 15 September 1935. Importantly for the investigators, these pages came from a limited run on that date for the Lancaster and Morecambe area. This was due to extensive coverage of the previous day's Morecambe carnival.

Police enquiries of the newspaper staff confirmed that 3,700 copies of that particular edition had been printed, and it was found that twenty-four had been sent to Ruxton's newsagent. The newspaper delivery boy was interviewed and he recalled that when he knocked on the doctor's door as he usually did, there was no response and so he put it through the letter box. This in itself was by no means conclusive evidence, but it added to the growing circumstantial case the police were building against the doctor.

The Ruxtons' cleaners, Mrs Oxley and Mrs Hampshire, provided police with details of the doctor's unusual behaviour in the days that followed the last sightings of Isabelle and Mary.

On Sunday 15 September, Mrs Hampshire started work in the Ruxton home at 4 pm. She found the doors to several rooms were locked and the bath was stained an unusual dirty yellow colour up to about six inches from the top. When she mentioned the stains to the doctor, he complained that Isabelle was lazy. However, Mrs Oxley confirmed that the bath had recently been cleaned by Mary, and on Saturday 14 September there had been no stains in it.

Mrs Hampshire also swept a great deal of straw from the stairs, from which the carpets had been removed. In the waiting room she found several pieces of carpet rolled up with a blue suit on top of them. In the yard she found more pieces of carpet, a bloodstained shirt, and two towels also soaked in blood; all of these items had been partially burnt. At 7 pm Mrs Hampshire called for her husband to

Isabelle Ruxton. Richard Seed

come and help her, and he scrubbed the stairs and landings. After the Hampshires had finished, Ruxton offered the blue suit to the other man and some pieces of carpet. He explained that the spots of blood on the suit were from his cut finger. The Hampshires accepted this offer and took the suit and carpet pieces home with them.

Overnight, it seems to have dawned on the doctor that he had made an error in allowing them to have his suit. He visited their home and asked Mrs Hampshire to burn it and watched as she did so. After he left, she washed the carpet pieces as they were bloodstained. Later that day, as her fears for the safety of the two women grew, she called at Ruxton's house and confronted him.

Mary Rogerson. Richard Seed

2 Dalton Square was the scene of two murders and the dismemberment of the bodies.
Richard Seed

He assured her that they were in London, but she accused him of lying. He then said that Isabelle had left him for another man. Although far from satisfied she felt there was little else she could do.

Mrs Oxley also provided information about the doctor's behaviour that helped to build the case against him. On 15 September he called at her home to say that Isabelle had gone to Edinburgh. The following day she arrived for work at his house at 7 am but found it empty. She returned at 9.15 am to see the doctor pulling up outside in his car. She noticed that his hand was bandaged, which he said was due to an accident with a tin opener.

Over the next few days his behaviour became increasingly suspicious, and during this time she saw a pile of burnt items in the yard, which had not been there on the previous Saturday. She also found bloodstains on a curtain at the top of the stairs. When she pointed this out to Ruxton, he cut them up, before burning the bloodstained piece and giving the remainder to his cleaner, so that she could make rags out of them. She was able to enter some rooms that had previously been locked, and noticed a peculiar smell in some of them. He also lit several fires in the yard and burnt a number of items but she could not make out what they were.

After the discovery of the bodies, and it was established that they were of two women, Ruxton was questioned by the police. Initially he was told that it was routine, and he seemed to think that he had convinced the police with his story about the two women having travelled to Edinburgh. Clearly, however, his behaviour in the preceding days took on a new and more sinister significance. The rumours grew and the doctor telephoned the Chief Constable to demand that the police issue a statement absolving him of any blame, and to confirm that he was not a suspect. However, unbeknown to him, the police had interviewed several people and had built up a case that they felt meant they could arrest him. This was to be supported by ground breaking forensic work that would be produced at his trial.

However, they knew of his violent temper, and the police were also aware that he had a revolver, quite legally, in his house.

Lancaster Town Hall, in which the Chief Constable had his office, where Ruxton was arrested. The author

THE ILLUSTRATED POLICE NEWS

DOCTOR ACCUSED OF MURDER

FATHER OF GIRL BREAKS DOWN IN BOX

DRAMATIC MOVE IN RAVINE CRIME

SEARCH FOR MISSING WIFE

Following conferences in Lancaster between local police officers and detectives from Scotland who are engaged on the mystery of the two dismembered bodies in the ravine at Moffat, events came with dramatic swiftness.

After spending several hours in the police-station, Dr. Buck Ruxton, a well-known Lancaster medical practitioner, whose wife and nursemaid had been reported missing, was arrested and charged with the murder of the nursemaid.

The detectives are confident that they will soon identify the second body, and they began a widespread search for the torso, which is still missing.

Ruxton was taken by surprise when arrested. The Illustrated Police News

To avoid the possibility of a potentially lethal confrontation, Chief Constable Vann decided to act as though he was going along with the doctor's request. He telephoned Ruxton on 13 October to express sympathy for the position he was in and invited him over to his office at the town hall. He assured the doctor that he would help him, and Ruxton must have felt pleased with himself as he made his way to the Chief Constable's office.

On his arrival, this was shattered as he was immediately arrested and charged with the murder of Mary Rogerson only. He was brought before the magistrates the following day, but such was his popularity, especially amongst the poor of the district, that many of his patients refused to believe him guilty, and continued to attend his surgery in the hope of persuading the authorities to at least grant him bail.

This was not agreed to and his trial began at Manchester Assizes on 2 March 1936; by this stage he was charged with the murder of his wife only. The prosecution alleged that he murdered both women on Sunday 15 September. He murdered

Isabelle in a jealous rage, and as this had been witnessed by Mary, she was murdered as a result. Over the following days he dismembered their bodies in the bath at 2 Dalton Square, and for part of that time he was wearing his blue suit, and despite his knowledge and skills, some blood spilled on the carpets and on the curtain at the top of the stairs.

THE ILLUSTRATED POLICE NEWS

RUXTON MURDER TRIAL

K.C. Alleges Doctor Planned Perfect Crime

UNFOUNDED JEALOUSY SUGGESTED

The prosecution alleged that Ruxton murdered Isabelle in a jealous rage. The Illustrated Police News

After leaving the children with his dentist friend, he had driven several times to the spot where the bodies were found. He had first removed identifying features such as finger tips, which had been burnt in his yard, together with other body parts.

It was thought that Isabelle may have discovered that he had a wife in India, which led her to become distraught at the thought of her children therefore being illegitimate. She may have threatened to expose him as a violent liar and that it was fear of such exposure that led him to kill her. However, it is more probable that he was in a jealous rage at the time, due to thinking, mistakenly, that she was having an affair with local man, Robert Edmondson, an assistant solicitor in the Town Clerk's department of Lancaster Corporation. He had known the Ruxtons since March 1934, and the doctor seems to have convinced himself that he and Isabelle were seeing each other behind his back.

The weekend before the murders, Isabelle had accompanied Edmondson, his sister and their parents on a trip to Edinburgh. It was established that separate rooms had been booked and there was no evidence to support Ruxton's suspicions. However, he had secretly followed them to the *Adelphi Hotel*, where they stayed, and he was certain that they had slept together. The prosecution believed that Ruxton had confronted her but had not believed her denial, and killed her.

At an earlier committal hearing, as Edmondson gave his evidence there was a violent outburst from the dock as Ruxton, rising to his feet, screamed 'Liar. Rogue. Blackguard. You home breaker. May the curse of my three children be on you.' However, later, at the trial, the judge told Edmondson that he was blameless and that his reputation remained intact.

The trial, which lasted between 2 and 13 March 1936, was however, to be remembered for the ground breaking forensic evidence that was given. The judge was Mr Justice Singleton; the prosecution was led by J C Jackson and the defence was conducted by Norman Birkett. The Edinburgh team had managed to reassemble both bodies, and Number 2, that of the older woman, was the most complete. Nowadays it would be much simpler to identify the remains and the causes of death, but it was much more difficult in the 1930s.

It proved possible to obtain helpful fingerprints from Number 1 and comparisons with prints in her room and on her belongings confirmed they were those of Mary Rogerson. This was the result of pioneering work by Detective Lieutenant Hammond of the Glasgow police, who spent eleven days in the Ruxton house trying to find a suitable set for comparison. The four distinctive vaccination marks also helped prove her identity. Nevertheless, it could not be shown how she died so it was decided to charge him with the murder of his wife only.

The crown claimed that the fact that Isabelle's head had been scalped, the lips removed together with the eyes and ears suggested that she had been asphyxiated as a result of manual strangulation. Those parts had been removed as they would have demonstrated that this had been how she was murdered.

As he was being sentenced to death Ruxton showed no emotion in the dock. The Illustrated Police News

THE ILLUSTRATED POLICE NEWS

Ruxton Sentenced To Death

CONDEMNED DOCTOR
HEARS HIS FATE
UNMOVED

The crown also used a pioneering process by which a photograph of the head was superimposed onto a portrait of Isabelle to provide confirmation of her identity. Local photographer Cecil Thomas had photographed her in early 1935; the conditions under which she was photographed were replicated in his studio, and the same camera and lens were used to photograph the head of Body 2. There was a perfect match, leaving little doubt as to whose body it was.

The doctor attempted to explain the blood in the house as being the result of Isabelle's miscarriage in 1932, and the blood on his blue suit as being due to his wearing it whilst assisting his friend at dental operations. The jury was not convinced and after deliberating for one hour, they found him guilty.

Following the imposition of the death penalty he was removed to the condemned cell at Strangeways, where he remained until his appeal was heard on 27 April 1936. He insisted on appearing in person as this vain man told a friend that if the appeal judges saw him they could not help but be impressed and thus realize he could not have committed these crimes. The appeal was based on the claim that there had been insufficient evidence to convict him. This was rejected by the court and he was hanged on 12 May 1936.

Six thousand people signed a petition for a reprieve, many of them from Lancaster, who could not believe he could have committed such terrible crimes. However, all doubts were removed on the Sunday following the execution, when the *News of the World* published a handwritten admission of guilt. Ruxton had handed the letter in a sealed envelope to a friend who visited him the day after the arrest. It read as follows:

I killed Mrs Ruxton in a fit of temper because I thought she had been with a man. I was mad at the time. Mary Rogerson was present at the time. I had to kill her.

B Ruxton

CHAPTER 10

John Smith
The Case of the Missing
Bullet
1941

I can't say owt, I didn't mean to kill her.

ohn Smith, a thirty-two-year-old mill worker was a single man, living with his mother at 44 Back Market Street, Shawforth. He began courting twenty-eight-year-old Margaret Ellen Knight, also a cotton operative, in November 1940. All seemed to be going well with the relationship in its early days, and Margaret invited him to her home at 609 Market Street, Whitworth, for Christmas dinner. They saw each other regularly, and by March 1941, Margaret was pregnant.

Margaret told her mother, Mrs Holt, who confronted Smith, when she saw him in a local shop. He told her that he was aware of her daughter's condition, and agreed to call at their home a few days later. He did so, as promised, and assured Margaret's mother and step-father that he very much wanted to marry their daughter. However, by this time, Margaret was beginning to have serious reservations, and initially refused to see him when he called at the house that night. She went into another room, but Smith persisted, and eventually spent several minutes with her. He emerged and informed her parents that Margaret had ended the relationship. She screamed after him, 'I will not marry him, I would rather die first'. Smith showed no emotion, but her rejection of him was to have devastating consequences.

Matters came to a head in a tragic and violent fashion on Sunday 18 May 1941. That afternoon, Margaret attended a meeting at Shawforth's Salvation Army Hall, with her friend, Doris Crossley. Five minutes into the meeting, Smith entered the hall and sat behind his former girlfriend. Two weeks earlier, he had joined the Home Guard and he was wearing his uniform, and carrying a rifle which he laid across his lap. The meeting drew to a close and Margaret and Doris left the hall, accompanied by Alice Shorrock, who had conducted the meeting, and who was also Smith's cousin.

Smith approached the three women, and as he did so, Doris turned to speak with another friend who was behind her. Smith and the other two women continued walking, and as they did so, he turned to Margaret and said 'What have I told you about coming here', to which she countered 'That's my business, not yours'. Alice then told him 'Don't be daft'.

The two women walked on, but Smith stayed where he was. A horrified Doris watched him raise his rifle, take aim at Margaret's back, and fire. Margaret screamed and fell to the ground. As she did so, Smith dropped the rifle and started to run away. However, the incident had been witnessed by Constable Duncan, who shouted 'Don't run away, it's no good.' Smith must have realized it was pointless to try to do so, and walked back towards the policeman. He said to

Doris 'I have done it, but I didn't think anything was in the rifle.' His mother, who had also been at the meeting now arrived on the scene. She was frantic and he attempted to calm her by saying 'Come on mother, it's an accident.' He turned to Constable Duncan, saying 'I didn't mean to shoot her.'

Margaret was still alive, and Dr Tierney was called to the scene. Despite his efforts to save her, she died shortly afterwards.

Margaret Knight. Manchester Evening News

H.G. Accused of Shooting "Army" Girl

Smith was detained at the scene of the shooting. Manchester Evening News

Smith was taken to Whitworth Police Station, where he was interviewed under caution by Inspector Ward. However, Smith limited himself to a simple statement 'I can't say owt. I didn't mean to kill her'. The following morning, however, he asked to make a statement, which read as follows:

I have asked to make this statement to make an early explanation, giving what has led up to this trouble. I started courting Margaret Knight at the back end of last year. We were very happy until a few weeks ago, when she told me she was finishing with me. This upset me very much. Some time later, I was told she had given over with me because she was afraid I would get her into trouble. I saw Margaret several times after and asked her about it, but she always gave the same answer 'no'. Through Margaret giving me up I was very upset, and worried about what was being said about me. On Sunday morning I thought I would get the gun to frighten her. After dinner I went out of the house, taking the gun with me. I called at the Salvation Army, and she was there.

On coming outside, I spoke to her and she would not speak back. After she had walked on a short distance, I fired the rifle meaning to aim over her head, meaning to frighten her. I was horror stricken when I saw her fall to the ground. Being so afraid, I turned and ran away. I have only been in the Home Guard about a fortnight, and up to the time of me using it to frighten Margaret I had received no instructions regarding loading and firing and it hitting her was an accident. I am very very sorry for what occurred, I did not intend to kill her.

The inquest into Margaret's death opened on the afternoon of Monday 19 May, at Hallifold Congregational School, Whitworth, before the county coroner, Stanley Turner. The only evidence offered was that of identification, which was provided by her step-father, Fred Holt. The inquest was adjourned so the police could conclude their enquiries.

The committal proceedings were held one month later, with the prosecution being conducted by H Riches, and the defendant being represented by A S Coupe. The crown did not accept that the killing was accidental. It was acknowledged that the accused had only been in the Home Guard for two weeks at the time of the killing, but it was untrue to suggest he had received no rifle training; he had in fact been given half an hour's instruction on the day before the shooting. This was admittedly only a limited amount of tuition, but it had been sufficient, argued Mr Riches, to enable Smith to load, take aim and fire the weapon.

Members of the Home Guard were called as witnesses by the prosecution, the first of which was window cleaner James Nightingale, of Market Street, who was the accused's corporal, responsible for instructing new members in the use of rifles. Coincidentally, the killing took place outside of his house, and on hearing the shot, he ran out. There he had met Smith who said to him 'I didn't mean to do it Jim, we were having a tiff.' He testified to the court that he had issued Smith with a rifle, and had given brief instructions in loading, unloading and operating the safety catch. In response to questions from the defence, the corporal said that he did not think that Smith had appeared to understand it all and seemed 'just as numb as before'. He also confirmed that Smith had never fired the rifle on the range.

The next witness was Sergeant Leonard Bell, of Smith's battalion. He had issued to each member, including the accused, five rounds of ammunition, with instructions that they must not load their weapons unless specifically ordered to do so by an NCO, and the ammunition was to be carried in their pockets.

Sergeant Major Grenville Barlow informed the court that on 17 May he had been responsible for checking the returned ammunition. Smith's clip contained only four rounds, and he could not account for the missing one, other than claiming that he must have lost it. The seriousness of this had been emphasized immediately, and he was ordered to report to the Commanding Officer at Company Headquarters on 20 May, when the nature of any disciplinary action would be decided. He was also ordered to return the bullet should he find it in the meantime.

Alleged to Have Put on Uniform and Shot Girl

H.G. DENIES CHARGE

Smith was alleged to have worn his uniform so that suspicions would not be aroused when he was seen carrying a rifle. Manchester Evening News

JOHN SMITH (32), of Back-street, Shawford, who was accused at Manchester Assizes to-day of murdering his former sweetheart, was alleged to have put on his Home Guard uniform when he was not on duty, gone out with his rifle, and shot the girl.

Sergeant Major Barlow also testified that Smith was not on duty on 18 May, the day of Margaret's killing, and accordingly had no right to be wearing his uniform, or to be carrying the rifle in public. The prosecution argued that he was wearing the uniform deliberately, so that people would not become suspicious when they saw him carrying the weapon, as if he had been in civilian clothing suspicions would have been raised.

The post-mortem had been conducted by Dr James Webster, who found that the only evidence of violence was that caused by the bullet wound in her back and at the front of her body, as it had passed through her. It had taken a downward direction, as the level of the exit wound was one inch below where it had entered. The doctor also confirmed that Margaret had been five months pregnant at the time of her death.

The prisoner was committed for trial at the next Manchester Assizes, where the prosecution was determined to present Smith as a cold calculating murderer, who killed his former sweetheart because she had rejected him. The trial took place on Tuesday 8 July 1941 before Mr Justice Hallett, with the prosecution being conducted by N K Laski and E Wooll. Smith was defended by J C Jolly and K Burke. It began at 10.30 am and ended at 8.30 pm.

The prosecution called the same witnesses that had appeared at the committal hearing, and highlighted several weaknesses in the defence case. The crown questioned why was the accused wearing his uniform and carrying his rifle on the day of the murder, when he was not on duty, and not entitled to do so;

how could the bullet, which had supposedly been lost and was not in the rifle when he returned it to his superiors in the Home Guard, get into the weapon, especially as he had been ordered not to load it; why was the trajectory of the bullet downward when he had claimed he attempted to fire above her head; and why had he chosen to attend the Salvation Army Hall that particular day, when he very rarely attended services there.

The defence decided to provide a different account of events to those previously given and called the prisoner to testify on his own behalf. Smith admitted being hurt by what Margaret had done to him, and he had been thinking of a way to frighten her, as an act of revenge. He insisted that he had indeed lost the fifth bullet, but later found it in his pocket. To forestall any disciplinary proceedings he decided to return it to his supervisors at the Home Guard that Sunday afternoon. This was why he decided to wear his uniform, and it was also why he was carrying the weapon. He had called at the Salvation Army Hall to let his mother know that he would be late home for his tea. It was only after arriving at the meeting that he decided he could frighten Margaret by firing the rifle above her head. As he took aim, and pulled the trigger, he described the rifle swivelling about in his hand, which meant the bullet did not go where it was aimed.

This claim to have killed her accidentally, led the defence to call on the jury to return a guilty verdict to the lesser charge of manslaughter. This call went unheeded and after deliberating for forty minutes he was found guilty of murder. However, the jury added a strong recommendation for mercy, before he was sentenced to death.

The appeal against conviction was heard on Wednesday 20 August 1941 at the Court of Criminal Appeal before the Lord Chief Justice, Lord Caldecott, sitting with Mr Justice Hawke and Mr Justice Humphreys. The defence argued that there had been insufficient evidence to support a guilty verdict to murder, and that the trial judge had not placed sufficient emphasis in his summing up on the option of a conviction for manslaughter.

The appeal was dismissed without the crown being required to make any form of address to the court. Mr Justice Hawke

SHOT SWEETHEART

H.G. is Hanged at Strangeways

JOHN SMITH, a 32-year-old cotton operative and member of the Home Guard, of Shawforth, Lancashire, was executed at Strangeways Gaol, Manchester, to-day for the murder of Margaret Ellen Knight, (28), his former sweetheart, at Whitworth, near Rochdale.

delivered the decision, and pointed out that the judge had told the jury to give consideration to the alternative charge of manslaughter, but they had rejected it.

The appeal having failed, there was to be no reprieve, and Smith was hanged by Thomas Pierrepoint in Strangeways on Thursday 4 September 1941, one of only three men hanged in the gaol during the Second World War.

The trial jury decided that Smith was guilty of deliberately murdering Margaret, and that her death had not been an accident. Manchester Evening News

Chapter 11

James Galbraith
Murder at the Docks
1944

The defence was asking the jury to accept that their client had stolen Walter's money, but that the murder had been committed by someone else.

During the evening of Saturday 8 April 1944, Third Officer Burnett Estill, on board the merchantman *Pacific Shipper*, berthed in Salford Docks, and went to the bridge to turn off a light. To do so he had to pass the cabin of the ship's Chief Wireless Operator. He noticed that it was locked, and that there was an unpleasant smell in the vicinity. He was unable to trace the source and returned to his own cabin. Sometime later, at about 11 pm, Estill went to the toilet, which was situated immediately below the Wireless Operator's cabin. He noticed a small quantity of blood on the toilet floor, which had trickled through the ceiling. He saw a patch of blood above his head and immediately informed the Chief Officer, who had a key to the cabin. The two men made their way to the cabin, and upon unlocking the door they discovered the body of James William Percey, the forty-eight-year-old Canadian Chief Radio Officer; the blood noticed by Estill in the toilet had flowed from several severe head wounds.

Percey had last been seen alive on the afternoon of Thursday 6 April, in the company of a younger man, dressed in a Chief Steward's uniform. The pair had been seen on Trafford Road, close to the docks, between 2 and 3 pm, and later on board the *Pacific Shipper*. They were subsequently seen drinking beer in Percey's cabin.

Salford Docks. Salford Local History Library

When the police enquiries began, they soon discovered that the key to the victim's cabin was missing from his key ring. As it was more than likely that the killer had removed it to lock the cabin behind him, it was seen as being an important piece of evidence. It was distinctive and a detailed description was given to the local press. It was stamped on one side *Eagle Lock Company, Cherryville, Conn, USA,* and on the other side were stamped the letters *LPCNT.*

The post-mortem was performed by Dr R W Wyse, resident surgical officer at Salford Royal Hospital. He concluded that death must have been instantaneous due to a fractured skull. This had been caused by several blows to the head with a heavy instrument. From the state of the body's decomposition, he determined that the victim could not have been alive after the previous Thursday evening.

The fatal blows had been done with an axe, which was found under the mattress of the bunk in the adjoining unlocked cabin.

Trafford Road, where the victim was seen shortly before his death, with a stranger dressed in a Chief Steward's uniform. Salford Local History Library

This was the Second Wireless Operator's, and he had been on leave at the time of the murder. Also with the murder weapon was the victim's missing key.

The police were able to trace the victim's movements in the days preceding the crime. He had travelled to Liverpool to collect money that was owed to him, and this was paid out on 3 April. He received back pay of £21 11s 10d from the Marconi Marine Company, and £66 18s 4d, which was compensation owing for loss of personal property, which he had lost when a previous ship he was on was sunk by a German torpedo. The £66 was paid out from a batch of new notes, numbered within the series A88 E514001 to 514500. When Percey's body was discovered he was in possession of just four shillings.

He was away from the ship on 4 and 5 April, and the morning of the following day. It was later that afternoon that he was seen, the worse for drink, on Trafford Road accompanied by the younger man in a Chief Steward's uniform. Later, the two of them were seen in the deceased's cabin, which was the last occasion upon which Walter was seen alive.

The police had several good descriptions of the mystery steward, and they quickly identified twenty-six-year-old James Galbraith of Moss Road, Stretford, as their prime suspect. He was arrested at his home in the early hours of Wednesday 12 April and when charged with the murder, he initially denied all knowledge of the crime, and protested his innocence. He continued to do so when he appeared later in the police court, and when asked if there were any reasons why he should not be remanded in custody, he replied 'The only reason I have is that I didn't kill the man, and I don't know anything about it.'

Nevertheless, the police built up a strong case against him and robbery was considered to be the motive. It was believed that the two men were not known to each other, but that Galbraith had engaged the other man in conversation, and realised that the drunken man had received a windfall of cash. Prior to 6 April, the police discovered that the accused man had been very short of money; on 5 April he had to borrow ten shillings from a shipping pool official, and he was dressed in his steward's uniform as he was desperately searching for work on a ship.

However, within an hour of being seen in the deceased's cabin, Galbraith bought a coat for £7 at a local shop. He spent lavishly during the next few days, and the notes he used bore the serial numbers of some of those paid out to the victim, in Liverpool, just a few days earlier.

A woman by the name of Alice Hyde, of Fallowfield, came forward and informed the investigating team that she had travelled to Liverpool with Galbraith, at his expense, shortly after the murder was committed. They were in a hotel room, when he pointed out an account of the crime in a local newspaper, and he told her that he had been drinking with the victim quite recently, and although the description of the wanted man fitted him, he assured her that when he had left the cabin, Percey had been alive and well.

There was also some forensic evidence, which was found by Dr J B Firth, Director of the Home Office Forensic Laboratory at Preston. Two hairs found on Galbraith's clothing were similar to that of the dead man. A blood smear, on the cuff of Galbraith's coat was suspicious but there was insufficient to group it. Furthermore, Galbraith's fingerprints were found at the crime scene.

Galbraith's trial took place between 9 and 11 May 1944, and the presiding judge was Mr Justice Hibbert, the prosecution was in the hands of Neville Laski and F J V Sandbach, and the defence team comprised Edward Wooll and Percy Butlin.

When he was first arrested, Galbraith had denied any knowledge whatsoever of the crime, and insisted that he had never met the victim, nor had he been on the ship. As for the cash, he maintained that it was his own, and that he had drawn £4 from the shipping pool office, and that he had £7 in savings.

Key as Clue to Death in Ship

By A STAFF REPORTER

Initially the police could not find the key to the victim's cabin. Manchester Evening News

However, as the evidence against him grew, his version of events changed accordingly. The police could prove he was with the victim in Trafford Road, and later that he was on the ship and in Percey's cabin. The police were also able to prove that he spent about £40 in notes traceable back to the deceased.

Galbraith realized that these facts had to be explained, and at the trial, at which he decided to testify, his account had changed drastically. He acknowledged that he had met Percey, who was a stranger to him, on Trafford Road, on the day of the murder. The Canadian was tipsy and staggering along the road. As Galbraith passed him, the accused man said that Percey asked 'Can you tell me where number nine dock is? My ship is there, I want to get back to it'.

Galbraith was in no hurry and offered to take him back to his ship. A grateful Percey had invited his new companion to his cabin for a few bottles of beer. Galbraith accepted, as he said he not only wanted a drink of beer, but was also hopeful of getting hold of some cheap cigarettes. Once in the cabin, he saw the radio operator put some money in a drawer, and when he

There was sufficient evidence to commit Galbraith for trial. Manchester Evening News

THE WORLD IS FULL OF WILLING PEOPLE; e willing to help, and the rest willing to them!"

GOULBURN'S

a pride in belonging to the first category

Manchester Evening News

THURSDAY, APRIL 27, 1944

Still th

BIR

ock Murder: Ship Steward for Trial

was left alone for a short time, he decided to make the most of this opportunity and he testified:

> *I noticed a wad of notes lying in the left hand drawer. Percey sat down again. We were talking. Then he went out of the cabin. He left me drinking my beer. While he was out, seeing the money there tempted me, and I opened the drawer, and took a handful of notes out. I could not say whether I took the lot or not. I think there were some left. I had to do it quickly as he might be back at any moment. I didn't count the notes at the time, but when I did after leaving the docks, I found there was about £36. I stole the money but I never murdered Percey. I never used any weapon, and did not lay a finger on him. There was no need for me to touch him.*

His host had then told him that he had to get ready for a date at 6.30 pm, and the accused insisted that he then left and that Percey was still alive. He was drunk but standing and changing into a clean shirt. Galbraith left the ship, and he further insisted he had not locked the cabin door, and that the first time he had seen the axe was at the police station following his arrest.

The defence was asking the jury to accept that their client had stolen Percey's money, but that the murder had been committed later by someone else, after Galbraith had left the

scene. The jury took just fifteen minutes to decide that this was not the case, and he was convicted of murder. As the death sentence was being passed, the judge asked if he had anything to say, to which he replied 'Only that I am not guilty of his murder.'

Galbraith appealed against his conviction, and this was

Number 9 dock, where the victim's ship was berthed. Salford Local History Library

Manchester Evening News
WEDNESDAY, APRIL 26, 1944

Ceiling Spot Led to Docks Discovery

PADLOCK ON DOOR OF CABIN

The victim's injuries had been so severe that blood seeped through the floor into the room below. Manchester Evening News

heard on 14 July 1944. Mr Wooll again represented the now condemned man, and suggested that although robbery had been proved, and that his client was guilty of that, no evidence had been presented that proved he had committed the murder. The trial judge was criticized for not pointing out that there had been sufficient time for the actual murderer to gain access to the cabin after Galbraith. He had also been unreasonable in allowing the jury to sit for nine hours on the final day of a murder trial, as the Galbraith jury had done, and then to be required to consider their verdict, and the many complex issues involved. Mr Wooll argued that their minds could not have been sufficiently receptive, and considered it was astonishing that the jury had taken just fifteen minutes in a case of what he considered to be exceptional difficulty.

The Lord Chief Justice, Lord Caldecott, dismissed the appeal and pointed to the overwhelming evidence against Galbraith. As for the third day lasting nine hours, he reminded Mr Wooll that the defence had not objected at the time. Furthermore, the jury had been asked by the judge if they wished to delay retiring to consider their verdict.

An application was made to the Attorney General for a certificate to appeal to the House of Lords. This was refused and Galbraith was hanged at Strangeways on Wednesday 26 July 1944, still protesting his innocence.

CHAPTER 12

Margaret Allen Rawtenstall's Lesbian Murderess 1949

... she met her end bravely, as well as any man ...

It was shortly after 4 am on Sunday 29 August 1948, and bus driver Herbert Beaumont was driving several colleagues home in a corporation bus. They had been attending a midnight meeting of Rawtenstall Corporation bus drivers, which had been called to discuss work schedules which were to be introduced arising from new services running to Bacup and Accrington. As he approached the junction of Bacup Road and Fallbarn Fold, he pulled to a halt to avoid hitting what he initially thought was a sack lying in the road. However, on leaving the vehicle, he was horrified to discover it was the body of an elderly woman, lying face down in the road, with her head resting on her folded arms.

The police and Dr F P Kay were on the scene within minutes, and the doctor's preliminary examination confirmed that there were significant injuries to the victim's head, and rigor mortis was complete. He could see no injuries to the rest of the body, and she had obviously not been the victim of a hit and run driver, as had been presumed. The woman had met her death elsewhere, and had been brought to the spot already dead. Confirmation was gained from a party of other bus drivers, who had left the meeting on foot; they had walked past the spot about thirty minutes before Herbert Beaumont, and the body had not been there then. The police quickly realized that they had a murder investigation on their hands.

The victim was sixty-eight-year-old Nancy Ellen Chadwick, who was well-known as a local eccentric, who dressed in old clothes, and who was also known as a fortune teller. She was also known to be rather miserly, and she was often seen on a park bench counting her money. She had property of her own from which she had an income, but in recent years she had acted as housekeeper to eighty-three-year-old John Whittaker of 81 Hardman Avenue. John was to become a second victim, as in the days that followed he found it difficult to come to terms with the

Herbert Beaumont, the bus driver who discovered the victim's body. Rossendale Free Press

death of his friend. Following a visit by a police officer to advise him that he would be required as a witness in the case, he calmly walked out of his home, saying goodbye to a neighbour; three hours later his body was discovered in a pond in which he had drowned himself.

The post-mortem on Nancy was performed by Dr Gilbert Barton later that Sunday. The victim was found to have been healthy for her age, and she was well nourished. Her hands, face and head were engrained with cindery dirt, the skin had been scraped from the fingers and thumb of her left hand, and her head was also matted with blood.

There were three large wounds and seven smaller ones to the head, all of which occurred before death. They had been caused by blows from a hammer-like instrument, and death was due to shock arising from these terrible injuries. The other marks to the body were consistent with her having been dragged, already dead, to the spot where she was found. She had been killed at least ten hours before the body was found, but he could not be any more specific.

A few hours after the body's discovery, the police began a thorough search of the immediate area, and this included the nearby River Irwell. Groups of interested spectators gathered along the bank of the river, watching the police officers peering into the water for clues. A helpful woman amongst the crowd shouted to one of the officers 'There is a bag in the water. Look it's down there'. She was pointing to a string shopping bag, which contained a leather handbag. A grateful officer thanked the woman, who was called Margaret Allen and who lived very close by. The bags were later identified as having belonged to the victim.

The following day the search for evidence continued, and as yet no murder weapon had been found. The search was extended to cover a wider area, and the celebrated Lancashire Police bloodhound Lubin, together with his handler, Sergeant Charles Smith, arrived from their Ribchester base. Lubin was given some of the victim's clothing to smell, and then set to work. Monday also saw the arrival of two Scotland Yard detectives to assist with the case; these were Chief Inspector Robert Stevens and Sergeant Campbell.

Appeals were also made seeking information about Nancy's movements, particularly on the day of her death. These were made in the press, by showing slides at local cinemas, and announcements on a local radio system, which served about 1,000 homes.

Police officers also made house-to-house enquiries, and one of these was at 137 Bacup Road. This was the home of the helpful Margaret Allen and it was directly opposite where the body had been found. She told the constable who called that she had heard nothing, before being awakened by the noise at the location after the body had been discovered.

Nevertheless, the police had discovered what appeared to be drag marks and traces of blood on the pavement outside of Margaret Allen's home, and their suspicions were aroused. She was visited again on 31 August by the police, and following a cursory search of her home, which yielded nothing useful, she made a statement. In this she acknowledged that she had known the victim for about one month and knew where she had lived. On Saturday 28 August she had called at 81 Hardman Street to see her, as she had promised to obtain some sugar for the older woman. Later that same day Mrs Chadwick had called at 137 Bacup Road and asked if she could come in, but this was not possible as Margaret Allen had to go out. She insisted that the victim had never been in her house and she had not seen her since that day. She also denied trying to rent one of her houses or having an argument with her.

However, there were inconsistencies in her statement, as police had spoken to Fred Taylor of 61 Hardman Street. He reported seeing Margaret Allen at about 9.25 am on the Saturday morning, which was the day before the body was discovered. He remembered speaking to her saying 'Hello Margaret, you are going to be lost up this way'. She had replied by telling him she had been to see Mrs Chadwick about renting a house, and had arranged to see her on the following Monday.

Furthermore, the police had been informed by Catherine Watson of Yarville Street close to Bacup Road that she had been sat in her front room, and she had seen Mrs Chadwick walking in the direction of Margaret Allen's home; she had also been carrying her string shopping bag. These witnesses proved that Margaret Allen had lied to the police, and she had in fact had recent contact with the victim, who on the morning of the murder, had been near to her house.

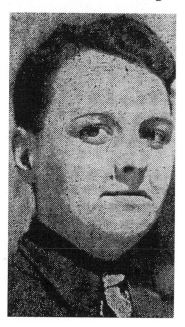

On 1 September, Inspector Stevens and his colleagues called again at 137 Bacup Road. The inspector challenged her with these discrepancies, and as he did so, a more thorough search was made of the premises. They found

Margaret Allen. Rossendale Free Press

a bag containing ashes and three rags, one of which was soaked in blood. She said that these were used to swab the floors. When the inspector asked when it was last used, there was a brief pause, after which she picked up her coat, and said 'Come on, I'll tell you about it.' She was cautioned, but she simply said 'Let's get out of here', and pointing towards the cellar she added 'That's where I put her.' At Rawtenstall Police Station she made a confession which read:

The other statements I have told you are wrong. What happened is this. I was coming out of the house on Saturday morning about 9.20 am, and Mrs Chadwick came round the corner. She asked if this was where I lived, and could she come in. I told her I was going out. I was in a funny mood and she seemed to get on my nerves, although she did not say anything. I told her to go and that she could see me some time else, but she seemed to insist on coming in.

She continued by saying that she and the older woman were inside the kitchen, and she noticed the hammer. She then described the murder:

On the spur of the moment, I hit her with the hammer. She gave a shout, which seemed to start me off more. I hit her a few times, I don't know how many. I pulled the body into my coal house. It was there all day.

She described going out soon afterwards to a local pub with her friend Annie Cook. Annie later confirmed that they had been at the *Ashton Arms*, and she described her friend Margaret as being a 'bit queer and she kept staring and giggling'.

The confession continued by stating that the killer had gone to bed at about 11 pm, but she could not sleep. She decided to drag the body to the river and throw it in. However, it was too heavy for her, and she abandoned it in the road, where it was discovered a short time later. A few minutes before that, she had taken the deceased's string shopping bag and its contents and thrown it into the river. It remained there until she pointed it out to the police. She disposed of the murder weapon by throwing the metal head into the river, and burning the wooden handle in her fire.

She insisted that she had not robbed Mrs Chadwick, and money had not been the motive. She concluded by saying 'I had no reason at all; it seemed to come over me. After she shouted it seemed to start me off'.

The statement was read over to her and she replied 'I did'.

Margaret Allen was forty-two years old and openly lesbian. She always dressed in men's clothing and was well known in the town's pubs, where she would often tell those willing to listen that she had had an operation to change her sex to that of a man. The twentieth child of a family of twenty-two, she worked in a cotton mill after leaving school. That was until war broke out, and in 1942, she began working as a bus conductress. She was happy in this work and was well liked by colleagues and passengers. This relatively happy period of her life came to an end in 1943, when her mother died.

This had a profound impact on her, and falling into an apparent depression, she failed to look after herself and her home. She failed to eat properly, but drank heavily and chain-smoked. She began to suffer from spells of dizziness and severe headaches. She was no longer able to work due to these complaints, and at the time of the murder she was receiving national assistance. Annie Cook would later describe one occasion when they argued and Allen had gone over to the gas oven and inserted the gas tube into her mouth.

Despite Allen's claims, the police were convinced that money had been the motive for the brutal murder. Allen admitted to them that she found it difficult to live on the limited income provided by her state benefits; she often had to borrow money from friends and acquaintances, and she could not always pay her household bills. Thus, considerable debts had accumulated; her weekly rent was just 6s 4d but her rent arrears were £15 4s; she had borrowed off several individuals.

Mrs Chadwick was known to carry quite large amounts of cash with her, and this could sometimes be as much as £30. The previous week, her nephew had given her a new leather purse with which she was delighted. She had shown it to a friend, Mary Ellen Jordan, the day before the murder, and it contained about £9. Mrs Jordan saw the old lady put it at the bottom of her handbag.

When the handbag was recovered from the Irwell, it contained a number of items such as private papers, playing cards, keys and spectacles. However, the purse was not there, nor was it found later, despite an extensive search of 81 Hardman Street and other locations. The police believed that Allen had taken the money and disposed of the purse.

The investigating officers realized that finding the murder weapon would certainly help them build a water-tight case. Allen told them that she had thrown it into the Irwell, and renewed efforts were made to locate it. Four army sappers with mine detectors tried to find it, as members of Rawtenstall fire brigade used pumps to lower the water level. An attempt was also made to divert the course of the river, by damming so that the area pointed out by the accused could be searched. However, despite all of these efforts, the weapon was never found.

As the trial at Manchester Assizes approached, the police still did not have a murder weapon, nor could they prove robbery to have been the motive. However, they had Allen's signed confession and an impressive amount of forensic evidence.

The incriminating rags, which had probably been used to try and clean up the murder scene, have already been mentioned. However, more evidence had been taken from the victim and

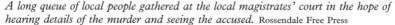

A long queue of local people gathered at the local magistrates' court in the hope of hearing details of the murder and seeing the accused. Rossendale Free Press

Single Human Hair as Exhibit

A total of 23 witnesses were called and there were 21 exhibits, ranging from samples of blood to a single human hair, and including ashes taken from accused's home and an overcoat belonging to the dead woman.

There was a great deal of incriminating forensic evidence. Rossendale Free Press

collected at 137 Bacup Road. Samples of the deceased's hair and blood, together with cindery dirt from her face, and fibres from her coat had been examined at the forensic laboratory in Preston.

In Allen's house, ashes from the fireplace proved to be similar to those on the victim's face; also in the ashes a strand of Mrs Chadwick's hair was found; and sand found in the fire place was also present on the victim's coat. Bloodstains were present in the coal cellar, and were also found on the front and back doors. It was realised that both victim and accused shared blood group O, but the stains were recent, and it was determined that they could not have been Allen's.

The accused's clothing was examined and blood was found on her shoes, trousers and blazer. Another strand of the victim's hair was found caked in some of this blood, and a fibre from the victim's coat was present on Allen's trousers.

The trial took place on Wednesday 12 January 1949 with Mr Justice Sellers acting as judge. The prosecution was undertaken by Dennis Gerrard KC, and C Leigh; the defence team comprised W Gorman KC and T M Blackhouse. A jury of nine men and three women was sworn in, as Allen sat impassively in the dock, flanked by two women prison officers. Allen was dressed in men's clothing as she had been at all of the hearings.

The prosecution was outlined by Mr Gerrard, and he began with the confession, which was followed by details of the forensic evidence. It was pointed out to the jury that it was not necessary to prove motive, and although the crown had no evidence that money was the reason behind the murder, details of the missing purse and the prisoner's financial difficulties were given.

The crown's most important witness however turned out to be Dr G A Cormack, medical officer at Strangeways. Allen had been under his care and observation since she was remanded in custody to the gaol. He had also interviewed her on several occasions. He told the court that there had been no history of severe physical illness, nor had there been a history of mental illness. In the prison, her behaviour had been normal, she had slept well, eaten normally, and was clean and tidy in her personal habits; she had been able to associate with others in the prison, and there had been no problems. Her memory and reasoning seemed good, and he was adamant that there was no evidence of mental illness.

When questioned by Mr Gorman for the defence, Dr Cormack acknowledged that Allen was going through the menopause. He agreed that at this time of their lives some individuals might do extraordinary things, and be quite normal afterwards. They might also experience dizziness and irritability. The accused however, had behaved normally whilst in Strangeways. The doctor concluded by stating 'In my opinion she would know what she was doing'.

Mr Gorman called no witnesses, and the accused did not speak in her own defence. He acknowledged that his client had indeed killed Mrs Chadwick, but he argued that Allen's state of mind had to be taken account of.

He urged the jury to ignore the possibility of money being the motive, as the crown had produced no evidence to demonstrate that the victim had money on her when she died, or that his client took any money. He also pointed out that there had been no evidence of any ill-feeling between the two women. He argued that the absence of any motive supported his claim that it was a senseless murder, which was committed due to insanity, exacerbated by her going through the menopause. He suggested that:

> There are secrets in the workings of the mind medical science has not yet revealed and it is for you as members of the jury, and you alone, to determine what was the state of mind of this particular woman when this event happened.

In conclusion, Mr Gorman made a valiant effort to persuade the jury that even the overwhelming forensic evidence was something that was actually in his client's favour. He suggested that shortly after the killing, Allen had left the house with incriminating bloodstains still present in the cellar, on the doors and on her clothing; she had also left blood stained rags in the house; furthermore she had left the body in the house all day, knowing that the victim would be missed. Finally, she had left the body almost immediately outside of her own front door.

When all of these factors were taken into account, he asked the jury to consider 'The purposeless fatuity and the madness of it' and to find that his client did not realise 'The mad passion of that violent act was a wrong thing'.

The judge's summing up focused on what had clearly been the main issue of the trial, and that was not whether the accused had killed the victim, but rather whether she had been insane when committing the act. He warned the jury that they could only make that decision on evidence presented at the trial, and not on an inference made by a non-expert. An individual was assumed sane until it was proven otherwise, and the onus for this rested on the defence. The jury members had to be satisfied that a killer was not in a position to know the nature and quality of what was being done, or of knowing right from wrong.

Insanity, he continued, was different from impulsiveness, emotional instability, hysteria and uncontrollability. He stated, ominously for the defence, that 'I must indicate that there is no evidence for your consideration on the vital matters which the law requires for this verdict to be given'. Indeed the only evidence regarding the relevant issues had been provided by Dr Cormack for the prosecution. No expert witness testimony had been given about the accused's state of mind at the time of the killing, by the defence.

The summing up lasted forty minutes, after which the jury retired for a further fifteen minutes, when they returned with the inevitable guilty verdict. After this, the judge sentenced Allen to death, before she was led out of the dock to the condemned cell at Strangeways; this was to be the last time she would be seen in men's clothing, as she would be required to dress in the prison's traditional striped dress, now that she was a condemned prisoner. The whole proceedings had lasted a little over four hours.

Allen's only visitor apart from her solicitor, Kenneth Yates, was Annie Cook, and she spent much of her time playing dominoes and cards with the prison guards. She was also allowed free cigarettes and beer.

Annie was allowed time off work by her employers, Glendale Yarns at Cloughfold, to organise a petition on her friend's behalf. Unfortunately, the response was poor, and despite two days making house-to-house calls, visiting pubs and work places, only 100 signatures were collected; a two hour spell on Rawtenstall market led to only four signatures being collected. She met with Mr Yates and they decided that it was not worthwhile forwarding the petition to the Home Secretary.

However, despite this initial setback, more signatures were gathered over the next few days, and the total reached 300. This hardly constituted overwhelming support from her hometown, but the petition was sent to the Home Secretary. Support also came from the town's MP, G H Walker, a lifelong opponent of capital punishment, who wrote a personal plea for a reprieve to the Home Secretary. This initial request was refused, as was the petition sent by Allen's solicitor. However, the local Labour Party members persuaded their MP to make a second attempt. He did, but this again was unsuccessful.

Local churches tried to help the condemned woman, and these included the Society of Friends, who met at Crawshawbooth. They sent the following telegram to the Home Secretary:

We, the Quaker Meeting near Rawtenstall, beg you to spare the life of Margaret Allen. We feel that the infliction of the death penalty is as great a crime as murder itself and we are deeply concerned at the effect such a penalty has on many sensitive souls.

Such pleas were not restricted to the Rawtenstall area, as Reverend Austin Lee, vicar of St Stephen's in Hounslow sent an impassioned letter to the King asking to spare Allen's life because of the terrible effect it would have on the prison officers concerned. He also wrote to the Queen suggesting that if the execution went ahead the male and female prison officers involved would be degraded and might be led to suicide and insanity at having to drag a woman to the scaffold.

As these futile attempts to save her life were made, Allen remained calm as she awaited her execution. Her final letter was to her friend Annie Cook, who had stood by her throughout the ordeal. She thanked Annie and enclosed her will which read as follows; 'I Margaret Allen wish to leave all my personal property to Annie Cook.' Included with the will were the following items: a cigarette lighter, cuff links, a small crucifix, a key, a collar stud, a ring, a padlock and 1s 6d in cash. All of her worldly goods accumulated over a lifetime, fitted into a registered envelope.

Allen had a final request to make of Annie, when they met for the last time in Strangeways on the eve of the execution. This was that Annie stand at the corner of Kay Street and Bacup Road, which was the spot they usually met if going for a drink or to do some shopping, at the moment she was being hanged. Annie agreed, and on the morning of Wednesday, 12 January 1949, Annie stood sobbing at the spot before making her way to St John's in Cloughfold, to pray for her friend.

There is an interesting postscript to the Margaret Allen case. The Royal Commission on Capital Punishment was sitting in early 1950, and was taking evidence from a number of witnesses, one of whom was Reverend A J Walker. He was the vicar of Tushingham, but until two months previously he had been chaplain at Strangeways Gaol. There he had witnessed six executions, five of which had been of men and the other was of Margaret Allen. Reverend Walker was one of those who felt strongly that women should not be hanged, no matter what the circumstances of their crimes. His description of Allen's execution to the Commission makes it clear that she was not dragged screaming to the scaffold. He said she met her end bravely as well as any man, and after a brief pause he added 'In fact better than any man.'

I somehow think that if she could have heard these comments she would no doubt have been quite pleased.

CHAPTER 13

Nenad Kovacevic
Old Scores Settled
1951

His last words to his solicitor were 'Look after Liza'.

At 7.20 am on Monday 9 October 1950, Alva Haworth, a platelayer, was walking along the Bury-Bacup railway track, just outside of Ramsbottom. He noticed that the door to the platelayers' hut was open several inches. He remembered that it had been closed when he last passed the spot on Saturday night, so he pushed the door open and inside saw the body of man lying with his head in the fire grate, and clutching a cap in his hand. He ran to his boss, William Crook, the foreman ganger at the School House in Shuttleworth, who contacted the police station in Ramsbottom.

Constable James Martlew called for an ambulance but was the first to arrive at the scene. A preliminary examination was

sufficient to see that the man had suffered severe head injuries, and on the floor he saw a number of strands of hair, all of which were matted in blood. The man was well dressed in a blue double-breasted pin-striped suit. He was over six feet tall and had long black hair. There was no sign of a struggle, but he noticed a bloodstained axe

Nenad Kovacevic. Bury Times

RAIL-CABIN MURDER: POLICE DETAIN MAN IN MIDLANDS

The police managed to intercept the bus on which the fugitive was travelling to London. Bury Times

on a shelf. He reported back to his superiors that they had a murder on their hands.

The scene was quickly filled with police cars and uniformed and plain-clothed police officers, under the control of Detective Chief Superintendent C N F Lindsay, chief of the Lancashire CID. Next on the scene was a team of forensic specialists from the Home Office Laboratory at Preston, led by Dr J B Firth. He discovered a layer of fine ash that had recently been deposited in the fire grate, which was identified as the remains of burnt paper. The body was taken to Bury, where pathologist Dr George Manning performed a post-mortem.

Although the body had not been identified he was of Eastern European appearance, and the police concentrated their enquiries on the surrounding towns of East Lancashire, in which many of the refugees from that part of the world were employed in the cotton and paper mills. By midnight of that day, the body had been identified as Radomir Djorovic, a Yugoslav national, who lodged in a house in Hamilton Street, Blackburn. The estimated time of death was given as during the afternoon of the previous day, Sunday 8 October. Other lodgers at the house advised the police that Radomir had arranged to meet a friend, Nenad Kovacevic, and that they were going to Edenfield on the Sunday afternoon. Kovacevic was traced to lodgings in Caton Street in Blackburn but he was not there when the police visited the house.

He was their prime suspect and his description was issued throughout the country. It was soon established that he had spent Monday night in bed and breakfast accommodation in Blackpool. Although he had left before the police arrived, it was discovered that he planned to take a coach from Fleetwood, which was travelling to London. This information was passed to the Staffordshire police force, who were aware of the route being taken by the Ribble Company coach. It was intercepted at Cannock, and an astonished Kovacevic was held at the local police station to await the arrival of Superintendent Lindsay and Detective Chief Inspector Melling of the Bury force.

When he was first interviewed by the Lancashire officers, Kovacevic initially denied knowing anything about the death. However, he did not keep this up for long, and within a short time admitted that he had indeed killed the other man. He told his interviewers 'I am sorry I killed Jack. I called Djorovic "Jack". He was my friend and I was crazy to do it. I was going to see my girl and had fixed a girl for Jack'. He continued by saying that they arrived at Edenfield on Sunday at 11 am, and it began to rain heavily. From the road they saw the hut by the side of the track, and decided to take shelter in it.

Once in the hut, they argued about events that had occurred in their homeland during World War Two, which ended with the prisoner hitting the other man with the axe that was already there.

Theirs had been an unlikely friendship, which had been formed when they met in the United Kingdom, where each of them had come in search of work after the war. Kovacevic was

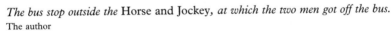

The bus stop outside the Horse and Jockey, *at which the two men got off the bus.* The author

The two men walked along this deserted path until they reached the railway line.
The author

born in 1921 in a small village, where his father was a major in the police force. In 1939, following Germany's invasion of Poland he was called up for military service, but was discharged one year later after his own country had been occupied by the Germans. He went into the mountains to fight the occupiers and joined the free force under the leadership of General Mihailovich, in which he remained until the Germans were driven out of the country by the Russians.

Whilst he had been serving under General Mihailovich, Kovacevic's father, two brothers and three sisters had been taken as hostages by the Germans, and were later summarily executed by their captors.

At the end of the hostilities he travelled through the mountains into Italy and stayed in a displaced persons' camp until December 1947, when he came to the United Kingdom. First of all he worked in a colliery but had to give this up on medical grounds, and was next employed in a brickworks in Derby. It was here that he first met Radomir, and both men then went to Blackburn to work in a local paper mill.

E.V.W. STANDS TRIAL ON MURDER CHARGE

Yugoslavs fought as soldiers in own country

The two men fought on opposite sides during World War Two. Bury Times

What made their friendship unusual was that Radomir had fought with the Serbian army, on the side of the Germans. Nevertheless, the two men appeared to have been able to put these differences to one side, although they occasionally argued about the war. Indeed, they seem to have got on well together, and on the day of the killing of Radomir, the dead man was being taken by Kovacevic to be formally introduced to a young woman named Ankia Mileusnic. The dead man had met her only once before, but wished to marry her. His friend Kovacevic had arranged the introduction, as was the custom in their country of birth. They had arrived early for this introduction and it was why they took shelter in the hut.

That Kovacevic had killed Radomir was not in doubt, but the motives offered for the killing were very different. The police maintained that robbery was the motive, but Kovacevic insisted that he had been provoked by the deceased man. The differing accounts would form the basis of his trial, which took place at the Manchester Assizes on Friday 8 December 1950 before Mr Justice Jones. The crown, represented by H I Nelson alleged that the accused man had decided to take advantage of the situation that arose when the two of them took shelter in such an isolated spot. The murder occurred so that the killer could rob him of his property, as he took his victim's raincoat, gloves, watch, cigarette case, wallet and cash. He had then burnt Radomir's papers in the fire in order to delay his identification.

Constable Denis Turner of the Staffordshire police force confirmed that when he arrested the accused, he had found the victim's belongings on him together with £6 7s 6d in cash. Chief Superintendent Lindsay testified that when he searched the victim's room he found no money, identity card or alien's certificate.

Djuro Seat, another countryman, who lodged with the dead man confirmed that he had seen him wearing the raincoat in question, on the morning of the killing, and that he had been with him on Saturday 7 October, when he had bought the gloves found in the accused's possession.

The prosecution also produced two Hungarian women, who were friends of the accused, named Elizabeth Seibert and Maria Lang, who were known as Liza and Bella respectively. They did not know Radomir, but had known Kovacevic for some time, and Kovacevic had hoped to marry Liza. The two young women testified that on the night of Sunday 8 October, the day of the killing, they were in Kovacevic's company. They visited several pubs in Blackburn, and he gave Bella a cigarette case, which was later identified as being the deceased's.

He also offered Liza a gold watch, which had no strap, but he promised to have one put on for her. The watch was later identified as having belonged to the victim, and had been found in the prisoner's possession. The prosecution later called Dora Williams to the stand, who was manageress of H G Riley's jewellers shop on the promenade in Blackpool. She testified that on Monday 9 October, Kovacevic had entered the shop, and ordered a leather strap to be put on the watch. She recalled the two metal 'ends', which she had to remove, and which had indicated that a metal bracelet had been taken off.

Mary Alice Birtwistle was an usherette at a Blackburn cinema, who with her husband Bernard, took in lodgers to supplement the family income. One of these was the defendant, whose weekly rent was fifteen shillings. However, by Saturday 7 October, he was ten shillings in arrears, but on the following evening at 6 pm, the day of the murder, he gave her £1. She next saw him at 10 pm, when he returned to the house with Liza and Bella. He had bought pork, tea cakes, slab cake, and beer which the five of them had for supper.

Bernard Birtwistle later testified that on the same evening, the prisoner initially offered him five shillings with which to buy himself some beer, but later increased this offer to ten shillings. At the end of the evening, the prisoner's two lady friends left in a taxi paid for by Kovacevic.

The crown contended that these witnesses gave support to the theory that robbery had been the motive for the murder. They had established that he had little or no money on the day before the crime, but on the evening of the murder he had plenty of money to spend on himself and others. He had also been found in possession of articles of his victim's clothing and he had offered the dead man's watch and cigarette case to Liza and Bella. The absence of the official documents that the deceased man was required to have, allegedly pointed to the accused having burnt them in the hut. There was no sign of a struggle and the prosecution insisted that the assailant had taken his victim by surprise.

The post-mortem was described by Dr Manning. The body was that of a well developed young man, aged about thirty years, six feet two inches in height. He had found nine wounds to the head and face, with severe bruising around both eyes. The skull had been fractured, and the cause of death was shock, stemming from the fracture to the skull, and haemorrhage. The victim had died about twenty-four hours before the post-mortem, which he had begun at 3 pm on Monday 9 October.

His defence counsel, Kenneth Burke, acknowledged that his client was responsible for the death of the victim, but his version of the circumstances leading to the death, was much different to that provided by the crown. He claimed that on the day of Radomir's death, they had got off the bus at the *Horse and Jockey* in Edenfield, with the intention of visiting his companion's prospective bride. However, as they crossed the bridge over the railway line it began to rain, and they decided to take shelter in the platelayers' hut. He insisted that at this stage he had no weapon and no intention of harming Radomir, who he suggested, would not have accompanied him to the hut if he had feared for his safety.

Once in the hut, the dead man took off his raincoat, which he hung up. There was no fire, and Radomir, who had some matches lit one, so they could dry themselves. At first their conversation focused on Radomir's possible marriage, but later they began to talk about the war. Radomir goaded him and asked 'Who was right?' The prisoner retorted that he had not been a collaborator; Radomir then suggested that if Kovacevic had not joined the freedom fighters, his family members would not have been slaughtered by the Germans.

They had argued about their respective roles in the war on previous occasions, but Radomir had always respected the prisoner's wish not to discuss the deaths of his family, as he found it so upsetting. On this occasion, however, Radomir had gone too far by raising the issue, which angered Kovacevic. This was made worse when Radomir started to laugh and said 'Don't think about those stupid things because it is all over now. You are not a woman.' He continued to laugh and ruffled Kovacevic's hair as though he was a little boy, before challenging him to a fight. He struck Kovacevic in the face, and they began to struggle. By now, Kovacevic was extremely angry. He picked up the axe, and used it to hit his companion twice on the head.

He realized that the other man was dead, and unable to look at the body, he took the raincoat off the hook to cover his eyes as he left the hut. At the time he did not know that the items he was said to have robbed were in the pockets. He insisted that robbery had not been the motive. He decided to travel to London, but intended to eventually surrender to the police. His defence was that he had been provoked into violence, and as a result, the jury could legitimately bring in a verdict of guilty to manslaughter.

In his summing up, the judge advised the jury that they must decide whether the prosecution had demonstrated to their satisfaction that the accused had intended to kill the victim or at least inflict grievous bodily harm. Regarding the defence claim that he was provoked, the judge stated:

We must be practical about these things. There are in this country, unfortunately, at the present time, very many people who have suffered terrible bereavements of that kind. It will probably occur to you as men and women of the world that it is hardly possible, if any one of those persons commits a crime, for the fact that he or she had relatives murdered by Russians or Germans to be put on as an excuse for the crime committed.

These sentiments probably reflected the fear that old scores would continue to be settled by violence in the United Kingdom, if people felt that the full force of the law would not be applied in such cases. The jury retired for seventy-five minutes and returned with a guilty verdict. When asked by the judge if he had anything to say, Kovacevic replied 'I cannot say anything. I killed him.'

The subsequent appeal, at which the condemned man was represented by Mr Christmas Humphreys, was heard before the Lord Chief Justice, Lord Goddard. Mr Humphreys argued that there had been clear evidence of provocation and that the trial judge had not provided the careful direction on the matter which the case required.

Lord Goddard did not require the crown to respond, and pointed out that the question of provocation depended entirely on the word of the condemned man. What had been proved beyond any reasonable doubt was that Kovacevic had killed his victim, with an axe of considerable size, and with great force. As far as Lord Goddard was concerned the trial judge had dealt with the provocation issue satisfactorily, and the motive had clearly been robbery. The appeal was dismissed.

Kovacevic, who had attended the appeal, was returned to the condemned cell at Strangeways Gaol, but his defence team, led by Bury solicitor, H C James, still hoped that a reprieve would be granted.

A petition containing more than 20,000 signatures was collected, and many of those who signed were his countrymen and women. Amongst those who signed was Pavle Markovic, by then a weaver in a Todmorden mill, but who had been the condemned man's commanding officer during the war. He told a *Bury Times* reporter 'I knew Nenad for three years. He was the bravest soldier I ever met'. He recalled one particular incident in which Kovacevic had made a single-handed assault on a German platoon, and took ten prisoners. Pavle concluded by

When sentencing Kovacevic to death, the judge made it clear that he believed a deterrent sentence was needed in this case. Bury Times

YUGOSLAV TO DIE FOR RAIL CABIN MURDER OF FRIEND

Pavle Markovic. Bury Times

saying 'It is all very tragic. I would give my life if Nenad could live.'

The leader of the freedom fighters to which Kovacevic had belonged, Drago Mihailovich, had been executed by the communists in his homeland four years earlier. However, his second in command, General Damjanovic, flew to the United Kingdom, especially to help with the appeal and to work on the petition for a reprieve. Another to offer his support to the campaign was ex King Peter of Yugoslavia, who sent a personal telegram to the King asking him to intervene. The campaign however was unsuccessful, and the execution was set for Friday 26 January 1951.

However, that was not quite the end of the story, for two days before the scheduled hanging, Kovacevic informed his solicitor, Mr James, that prior to the crime, he had lent a friend Peter Vramjas, £210, which would prove that he had money of his own and did not need to rob Radomir. The Home Office was advised, and despite being told that he was living in Birmingham, the police located him in Leeds, on the eve of the execution. However, he denied ever receiving the money.

On being advised of the failure of this last desperate attempt to avoid the noose, he arranged with Mr James to make a will,

Kovacevic was his mother's only surviving child. Bury Times

☛ YUGOSLAV TELLS OF TRAGIC NIGHT IN RAIL CABIN

'I SAID MY MOTHER LOST ALL ... AND NOW ME'

WEDNESDAY, JANUARY 24 1951

—Mother of— condemned man —disappears—

A FRANTIC eleventh hour bid is being made by Yugoslav authorities in Britain to trace the mother of 29-years-old Nenad Kovacevic, condemned to die on Friday, for the murder

Attempts to locate his mother and bring her to this country failed. Bury Times

in which he left all of his possessions to Liza. His last words to his solicitor were 'Look after Liza'.

Throughout the period of his contact with Kovacevic, Mr James had made frantic efforts to trace his mother in Yugoslavia. He managed to do so, and he tried to arrange for her to travel to see him before he died. Unfortunately she could not make the journey, and did not see him, the last of her children, who also met a violent end.

Kovacevic was hanged on schedule, on Friday 26 January 1951 and struggled every step from the condemned cell to the gallows. At 8 am however, he died, and on that cold winter morning his war was finally over.

CHAPTER 14

Louisa Merrifield
The Blackpool Poisoner
1953

Perhaps the most damning evidence presented by the crown, however, was that provided by several witnesses who claimed that they had heard Louisa Merrifield describe Sarah as being dead, several days before she actually died.

Sarah Ricketts was a seventy-nine-year-old widow, who lived alone at 339 Devonshire Road, a bungalow in the affluent North Shore district of Blackpool. Her life had been marked by tragedy, as her two husbands had both committed suicide by gassing themselves in the kitchen of the bungalow in which she still lived. The first had done so twenty years earlier, and the second had killed himself seven years later. However, each of them had left her enough capital to provide her with a reasonable private income, which was supplemented by rents from other property she owned in the town.

Sarah had lived alone for the past seven years, and after disagreements with her two daughters, and arguments with her neighbours, she was living almost as a recluse. She had a reputation for being argumentative and miserly, and although she suffered from bronchitis she was in good health for her age. She disliked housework however, and decided to advertise for live-in help.

Sarah Ricketts. Manchester Evening News

Sarah subsequently employed seventy-year-old Arthur Merrifield and his wife, forty-six-year-old Louisa, who moved into the bungalow on 12 March 1953. Louisa was the dominant partner in the relationship, and he was her third husband. She was the daughter of a miner and one of eight children. She had left school at thirteen years of age to work in the card room of a mill. When she was twenty-one she started work in the kitchens of a hospital in Ormskirk, before deciding to enter private service. She married for the first time in 1931, and had nine children before her husband died in 1949. She remarried in January 1950, and following the death of her second husband two months later, she married for the third time later that year, after which they moved to Blackpool, looking for work.

A little over one month after the Merrifields moved in to work for Sarah, the old woman died, on Tuesday 14 April. A doctor was called to the scene, but he refused to issue a death certificate, as he had seen her quite recently and she had been in good health. He advised the coroner and a post-mortem was carried out. This ruled out the possibility of natural causes and the police were called in. They were left with three possibilities, namely that her death had been due to an accident, suicide or murder.

The local police decided to call in the experts, and the Scotland

Louisa Merrifield. Manchester Evening News

Yard detectives Superintendent Colin McDonald and Sergeant Nick Carter soon arrived in Blackpool. They questioned Louisa Merrifield on several occasions, and on 17 April she provided them with her account of what had occurred in the bungalow in the preceding weeks.

Alfred Merrifield. Manchester Evening News

She claimed that the old lady had been ill and could not look after herself properly. There was very little food in the house when the Merrifields arrived, but there was a great deal of alcohol, as she was a heavy drinker; one of her favourite drinks was brandy with a raw egg in it, which she had three times daily. Louisa Merrifield insisted that when she and her husband started work for her, they assumed control of the household budget and began to ensure that Sarah was given a much better diet, such as fish and chicken. She had begun to look much better, but continued to drink heavily. Sarah then took back responsibility for the household finances, and stopped buying decent food, and began ordering large quantities of alcohol again. Soon there were deliveries of brandy, rum and Guinness to the bungalow.

She then described an apparent deterioration in Sarah's health from 9 April, and advised her to consult a doctor, but the old woman decided not to follow this advice. The Merrifields then tended to her needs on a twenty-four hour a day basis, but she became ill on Sunday 12 April and the following day. During this time she had no food other than raw eggs in brandy, together with several bottles of Guinness. Such was the deterioration in her health that the Merrifields called Dr Wood who could find nothing wrong with the old woman. Nevertheless, the Merrifields insisted that Sarah continued to drink heavily, and by 3 am on Tuesday 14 April her condition had worsened. Louisa Merrifield insisted that she sat up with her employer throughout that night. At 8.30 that morning she went to the surgery of Dr Page, but he was not available until noon. When he arrived, he suggested the Merrifields contact yet another doctor, who knew Sarah's history. This was Dr Yule, but by the time he arrived Sarah had died.

This account did not satisfy the police, and on Friday 1 May 1953 they charged her with the murder of Sarah Ricketts. They believed that their calling out several different doctors was an attempt to suggest that Sarah's health was deteriorating gradually, in advance of the murder, and hopefully avoid the need for a post-mortem.

She made a brief appearance before Blackpool Magistrates' Court that day, and as she was being led from the dock and into custody her husband shouted 'Keep your chin up Louie'. He left the court building waving his walking stick in a jocular manner to the crowd outside.

The accused made several such appearances, as she awaited committal for trial, and on each occasion, her husband was there, cheerfully giving his support. On 15 May however, he was in for a surprise. He was admitted into the cell area of the court to see her, but on this occasion, he too was arrested and charged with the murder of his former employer.

It was on 20 July 1953 that the Merrifields entered the dock of Manchester Assizes to face trial, represented by Mr Nahum.

The prosecution was led by the Attorney General, Sir Lionel Heald. He addressed the jury to explain why he was taking personal responsibility for prosecuting this particular case. He explained that although murder in any guise was of course extremely serious, murder by poisoning, which was alleged in this case, was considered to be particularly heinous, due to its special elements of secrecy and treachery. A senior law officer

Sir Lionel Heald. Manchester Evening News

traditionally appeared in such cases as a means of demonstrating the gravity of the alleged crime.

The prosecution case was that the Merrifields had poisoned their employer with Roedine, a well known rat poison, and their motive had been financial gain. A key plank in their case was that soon after their arrival, Sarah had changed her will, leaving her bungalow, valued at £4,000, to them.

The jury heard evidence surrounding the cause of death, which the crown argued, could not have been due to natural causes, although this would be challenged by the defence. Suicide and accidental death were discounted, as if either was the case, there would have been traces of the poison found in the bungalow, as there would have been no need for anyone to hide it.

Indeed, no trace of the poison allegedly used, was ever found, but the crown attempted to establish that a tin of Roedine, which was easily available, was purchased by the Merrifields, and that this was the means by which they murdered Sarah Ricketts.

Perhaps the most damning evidence presented by the crown however, was that provided by several witnesses who claimed that they had heard Louisa Merrifield describe Sarah as being dead, several days before she actually died.

To prove poisoning, the crown called Dr George Manning, who performed a post-mortem on 14 April, and chemist Alan Thompson, both from the North West Forensic Laboratory at Preston. Dr Manning found pin point haemorrhages on the victim's lips, mouth and tongue, together with haemorrhages on the lungs and on the surface of the heart. These indicated some abnormal condition of the blood vessels. The state of her liver suggested that some form of toxic change had taken place.

Mr Thompson had made an internal examination, and discovered .042 grains of yellow phosphorous in her stomach, and .099 grains in her intestine. He also discovered bran, which along with yellow phosphorous was found in Roedine. The crown argued that following Dr Wood's assertion that Sarah was in good health when he saw her, the Merrifields had poisoned her by administering Roedine either in one large single dose later that evening, or by giving her several smaller doses throughout the night. The yellow phosphorous found by Mr Thompson were the traces that had not been absorbed into the victim's body.

Yellow phosphorous however, has a distinctive garlic smell, so that it would have been immediately obvious to anyone taking it that some unusual substance was being administered. Dr Manning therefore, conducted some tests as to how the smell and taste might be disguised. Brandy, he discovered, masked the taste but not the smell. However, blackcurrant jam, a particular favourite of the victim, and which she often took on a large spoon without bread and butter, masked both the smell and the taste. The crown also presented evidence that the accused had purchased a tin of Roedine, and that it had been fed to their victim with blackcurrant jam, so that Sarah would not have known it was being given to her.

The sale of poisons was overseen by the Poisons Board, and those selling poisons had to maintain full records. Furthermore, those purchasing it had to provide proof of identity and an address, together with a signature. This meant that anyone buying poison could be traced easily. Roedine however, was not then covered by these regulations despite a one shilling tin containing enough yellow phosphorous to kill several people. It could be bought at any chemist's shop, and convinced that this was the means by which the

murder had been committed, the police visited every chemist in the North West of England. Harold Hague, who owned Cottons chemist's shop near Victoria Railway Station in Manchester, and his assistant Mavis Atkinson, were located by the investigating team. They were called to give evidence at the trial that Alfred Merrifield had purchased Roedine at the

Mr Nahum. Manchester Evening News

shop, before the murder occurred. If the crown could prove this to be so, it would be important to their case. However, the chemist and his assistant proved to be less than convincing witnesses at the trial.

An identification parade was held at Blackpool Police Station soon after the chemist and his assistant had been found, at which Alfred Merrifield and eleven other men lined up. Miss Atkinson did pause in front of the suspect, but neither she nor Mr Hague picked him out. It was only at the committal hearing in Blackpool Magistrates' Court, that both witnesses positively identified him as the man who had bought the rat poison at their shop.

At the trial, Miss Atkinson was again asked if the man who had bought the Roedine was present in the court. She immediately pointed to Alfred Merrifield in the dock and said 'The gentleman wearing the hearing aid', at which the prisoner smiled broadly. She was reminded of her initial failure to pick him out at the original identification parade, by Sir Lionel who asked her why she had not done so then, to which the witness replied 'I was too nervous'.

She was cross examined by Mr Nahum for the defence, and after initially denying having seen a photograph of Alfred Merrifield in the press after the first identification parade, she finally admitted having possibly seen one in a newspaper, but she denied vehemently the suggestion that this had influenced her decision to identify him later.

Mr Hague appeared next, and he too picked Alfred Merrifield out as a man who had bought Roedine at his shop. Under cross examination by Mr Nahum, he acknowledged that he too had failed to pick him out at Blackpool Police Station. He also stated that he had later seen several newspaper photographs of

Mavis Atkinson. Manchester Evening News

the accused man. Under further questioning he had to admit that he had told a police inspector after the initial identification parade that he could not be certain that the man who had been in his shop was in fact one of the twelve men in the line-up.

The crown's case had suffered a setback as the defence had destroyed their attempt to prove that Alfred Merrifield had bought a tin of Roedine. Later, when he testified in his own defence he was asked about this issue and when asked if he had bought a tin of the rat poison at the shop, he replied 'Definitely not. I've never been to Manchester for five solid years. I've never left the boundary of Blackpool for twelve months.' He emphasized the point by banging his fist down on the witness box, and shouting that it was 'Perjured evidence, all cooked up by Scotland Yard men.' The judge intervened and warned him about his conduct. This however, did not deter him, and he continued by shouting even louder 'This is a British court of justice gentlemen. I am giving my evidence in a fight for my life and my wife's.'

Despite this obvious setback for the crown, the Attorney General pressed on, and presented the jury with details of a handbag and spoon, which he said supported their claims. On the afternoon of 14 April, Louisa Merrifield left her handbag with a friend, which was later traced by the police. In it they found a spoon, which seemed to be out of place, and on which, the forensic scientist Alan Thompson found traces of black-currant jam. No evidence of yellow phosphorous was found on the spoon, but the crown alleged that this was the means by which the poison had been administered by the Merrifields.

The accused woman had left the handbag with Alice Hands, shortly after her employer's death saying 'It looks as if there is going to be trouble. There are policies in it, which I do not want Arthur to see.' There had been friction between the couple, as she was paying premiums on his life. He objected on the grounds that they cost too much, and she implied that she wanted the bag hidden from her husband rather than from the police.

As for the spoon, the accused woman told the police that she and her husband had moved several times, and she sometimes put small objects such as cutlery in her bag, and she told the police when confronted with the spoon 'I thought I took them all out, but it is possible one had been left in.'

The Attorney General then focused on the financial motive for the alleged crime. Within a short time of moving into the bungalow, Louisa Merrifield visited solicitor William Darbyshire to arrange for a new will to be made out for her employer. In it, Louisa Merrifield alone was to inherit the bungalow, but when it was signed, her husband's name was added in handwriting, as a joint beneficiary.

Her husband it seems did not want to be left out of this arrangement, but it annoyed his wife. On 13 April, she met an acquaintance, Elizabeth Barraclough and told her that on one occasion she had returned to find her husband in bed with Sarah. He had denied any impropriety, and claimed he was massaging her feet. However, Mrs Barraclough reported that his wife had told her 'If this goes on again, I'll poison the old woman and him as well.'

It might seem strange that within less than two weeks of the Merrifields starting work for her, she should make out a new will, making them major beneficiaries. There is no evidence of any pressure, and Mr Darbyshire confirmed that when he and his assistant visited her on 31 March, for her to sign the document, she was mentally alert and fully aware of what was going on, and there were no indications of her being under any kind of pressure. A few days later, Louisa Merrifield asked Dr Yule to visit the bungalow to confirm that Sarah was fit to make a new will. He was surprised at this request as the will had already been made out, but she explained that she was afraid the old lady might die unexpectedly, and she wanted to avoid any trouble with her relatives. The doctor did not make any formal assessment but asked Sarah about the new will, to which she replied 'I am looking after them that look after me.'

So why would the wealthy widow change her will voluntarily, making people she hardly knew, major beneficiaries? It emerged that she had changed her will on several occasions in the past, and it was believed that this friendless old lady, estranged from her family, used it as a device to ensure that the Merrifields, whom she liked initially, did not leave her. She seems to have found them a caring and helpful couple in the early stages of their stay, but these warm feelings were soon replaced by others which were less friendly. Sir Lionel argued that fearing dismissal and the loss of their inheritance the Merrifields decided to kill her before she had the opportunity of changing the will again.

Witnesses were called to prove that the Merrifields were aware of this change in her views about them. On the morning of 13 April, George Forjan, a delivery van driver called at the bungalow to deliver a bottle of brandy to Sarah. She opened the door and said to him 'I don't know what they're doing with my money. I can't pay you.' Alfred Merrifield was standing behind her, and also heard her say she was not being given adequate food and the couple would have to go. Another delivery man, Joseph Malone, who dropped off groceries, was also told by Sarah that the Merrifields were not feeding her properly.

One of the few regular visitors to the bungalow was Arthur Gardner who paid rent in cash to Sarah for one of her properties he rented on Broughton Avenue. He called on 11 April and she pointed to the Merrifields and shook her head, as though indicating that she was having problems with them.

So did the Merrifields believe that they were on the verge of being dismissed, and thus losing their inheritance? And if so, did this prompt them to poison Sarah?

The defence attempted to demonstrate that Sarah had not in fact died due to poisoning, but had died from natural causes. The most important witness for the defence was James Webster, Director of the Home Office Laboratory in Birmingham, and Professor of Forensic Medicine at the city's university. The witness was a highly respected and greatly experienced pathologist, who had testified at many murder trials, often on behalf of the crown.

Professor Webster testified that the so-called victim of poisoning had actually died from natural causes, namely of a necrosis of the liver, and that there would not necessarily have been signs of this even as late as the eve of her death. Furthermore, he claimed that this could have been caused from lack of food or a poor diet. The Merrifields claimed that they

Merrifield Q.C. agrees with judge—

'THIS COULD BE MURDER ATTEMPT'

IF poison was given but widow's death was natural

ATTEMPTED MURDER would be the proper verdict in the Merrifield trial IF the jury found that one or both of the Merrifields gave rat poison to Mrs. Ricketts, intending to kill her, but that she had died not of poisoning but of natural causes.

The defence hoped to persuade the jury that Sarah Ricketts had died of natural causes. Manchester Evening News

had been attempting to improve her diet, but Sarah had failed to co-operate and had resumed eating a poor diet and drinking heavily, thereby bringing about her own death.

Dr Webster argued that there was no evidence that any more yellow phosphorous than the 0.141 of a grain found at the post-mortem, had entered her body. Therefore it could not be said to have definitely been the cause of death. At this point the judge intervened and asked the professor to give his opinion as to how that 0.141 of a grain of the poison, had entered her body. Professor Webster had to concede that it could only have done so by way of her mouth, and furthermore, he conceded that Roedine was the most plausible means by which it had been taken in.

Nevertheless, the professor was adamant that there was no proof that this had accelerated Sarah's death; the only way it could have done was by causing shock, but there had been no signs of this.

The Attorney General sought clarification of the professor's conclusions and asked him 'What you have to postulate is this – which is she died just exactly at the moment before the final absorption of the phosphorous would have been taking place through the wall?' To this the witness replied 'I say that she died before there was any proof that the first particle of phosphorous had passed through the wall.'

Perhaps Professor Webster's testimony may have been sufficient to have planted seeds of doubt in the minds of some of the jurors, and led them to consider a lesser charge of attempted murder, but the crown produced a number of witnesses, who provided damning evidence.

David Brewer of Alexandra Road, South Shore, described a conversation with Louisa Merrifield as early as 25 March, a date he remembered as it coincided with his landlady's birthday. She had said to him 'Oh David, I've had a bit of luck. Where I have been living the old lady has died and left me her bungalow.' She had continued by telling the witness that she planned to sell the property and open up a nursing home on the South Promenade.

Jessie Brewer, of Warley Road, Blackpool, told the police that it made her 'feel all funny', when she read the newspaper reports of the old lady's death in the Sunday newspaper. She recalled meeting Louisa Merrifield on the afternoon of 11 April in the town centre, when the accused woman had grabbed her by the arm and said 'Mrs Brewer, we are landed. I went to live with an old girl, and she died and left me a bungalow worth £4,000.' She complained that it was to have been left to her alone, but her husband had interfered and had his name included in the will as a beneficiary.

On Sunday 12 April, two days before Sarah's death, Louisa Merrifield was visiting the home of Mr and Mrs Hands. Also present was Mrs King, who heard the accused say 'I'll be going as I have to lay the old lady out'.

Under cross examination from the Attorney General, she denied having said those words and insisted that what she had actually said was 'I will be going or the old man will be laying me out.' As for the other witnesses who testified she had spoken of the victim's death days before it occurred she dismissed them by suggesting 'I think it's just jealousy. They are all up to their necks in mortgage. I never said Mrs Ricketts was dead before she died, to anyone.'

She also denied ever having threatened to poison Sarah and her husband, as at one point the Attorney General even implied that he might have been a future victim, given the secret insurance policies she still had out on his life and her apparent frustration at not being the sole beneficiary of the will. Sir Lionel asked her 'Wasn't Mr Merrifield afraid of what you might do to one or both of them?' to which she replied 'No, he had no need.'

The trial drew to a close during the afternoon of the eleventh day, on Friday 1 August. The prosecution spoke of the attempts made by the Merrifields to create an impression of an old woman not eating properly and drinking to excess; to support this they called out doctors for what were spurious reasons. They had not forced their victim to change her will in their favour, but once she had done so, she might as well have signed her own death warrant. The crown also pointed to the various witnesses who had heard Louisa Merrifield talk of her then still alive employer as being dead. As for the claims made by Dr Webster, a disdainful Attorney General suggested that Sarah Ricketts might also have been struck by lightning.

In his closing speech Mr Nahum insisted that the yellow phosphorous introduced into the dead woman's body was not the cause of death, which had in fact been due to natural causes as suggested by Dr Webster. He even suggested that the source of the poison might well have been contaminated beer bottles from a brewery where rat poison was being used, and which had been purchased by the deceased.

In his summing up the judge advised the jury that if they were persuaded by Dr Webster's evidence and believed that the cause of death was natural causes, but Roedine had been administered by one or both of the Merrifields, then attempted murder was the most appropriate charge, and they could not bring in a murder conviction. He also emphasized that the evidence of Mr Hague and Miss Atkinson should be disregarded totally as they had both seen newspaper photographs of Alfred Merrifield between failing to identify him at the police station, and picking him out at the magistrates' court.

The jury retired at a few minutes before 4 pm and took five hours before returning with their verdicts. Louisa Merrifield staggered in the dock and had to be supported by a warder as the jury foreman announced they had found her guilty. The foreman then advised the judge that they could not agree on her husband, who was returned to the cells. He was heard to ask a warder what that meant and he was told he faced a retrial, probably in October.

The convicted prisoner was sentenced to death at 10 pm and was taken to the condemned cell at Strangeways gaol. An appeal failed and she was hanged on Friday 16 September 1953. As she awaited execution, Alfred gave an interview to the press in which he made some derogatory remarks about his wife, and she refused to see him. However, shortly before she was hanged, they were reconciled and he was able to visit her.

The crown decided not to retry Alfred, who died in 1962 after failing to gain ownership of the bungalow, although he was given a small sum in compensation by Sarah's daughters. He spent his last years scratching a living from telling anyone who would listen about his involvement in the case.

One is left to wonder whether his wife might not have avoided the noose and been convicted of attempted murder, had she not boasted to others about inheriting the bungalow and prematurely announcing her employer's death.

Sources and Bibliography

Smith, H Bodell, *The State Murder of John Griffiths & The Ilford Executions or Capital Punishment Condemned,* The C W Daniel Company, 1923
Glaister, John, *The Power of Poison,* Christopher Johnson, 1954
Glaister, John, and Brash, James Couper, *Medico-Legal Aspects of The Ruxton Case,* E & S Livingstone, 1937

Bury Times
The Guardian (Bury)
The Illustrated Police News
The Manchester Evening Chronicle
Manchester Evening News
Rossendale Free Press
The Standard (Oldham)

Index